Learning to Rock Climb

Learning

SIERRA CLUB BOOKS   SAN FRANCISCO

to Rock Climb

by Michael Loughman

Photographs by the author
Drawings by Rose Craig

The Sierra Club, founded in 1892 by John Muir, has devoted itself to the study and protection of the earth's scenic and ecological resources—mountains, wetlands, woodlands, wild shores and rivers, deserts and plains. The publishing program of the Sierra Club offers books to the public as a nonprofit educational service in the hope that they may enlarge the public's understanding of the Club's basic concerns. The point of view expressed in each book, however, does not necessarily represent that of the Club. The Sierra Club has some sixty chapters coast to coast, in Canada, Hawaii, and Alaska. For information about how you may participate in its programs to preserve wilderness and the quality of life, please address inquiries to Sierra Club, 730 Polk Street, San Francisco, CA 94109.

Library of Congress Cataloging in Publication Data
Loughman, Michael, 1938–
    Learning to rock climb.

    Includes index.
    1.   Rock climbing.   I.   Title.
GV200.2.L68   796.5'223   80-28639
ISBN 0-87156-279-0
ISBN 0-87156-281-2 (pbk.)

Book, jacket and cover design by Paula Schlosser

Printed in the United States of America on acid-free paper containing 50% recovered waste paper

20   19   18   17   16   15   14

This book is humbly dedicated to those people who invented free climbing as I know it. I have known them only fleetingly, but such as I have to offer here that is worthwhile has come from them.

To Glen Dawson, Chuck Wilts, Royal Robbins, Mark Powell, and Chuck Pratt.

Contents

Acknowledgments

Maria Cranor, Tom Higgins, and Debra Smith read the first draft of the manuscript, took hearty exception to some of my pronouncements, and made many suggestions for improvements. Rob Loveman patiently instructed me in the kinetics of belayed leader falls, a subject which turns out to be much more complicated than has been acknowledged in the literature. Any physical errors or misconceptions are strictly my own. Diana Landau of Sierra Club Books questioned my text at every turn, and although it was a trying experience for both of us, it led to major improvements.

Rose Craig helped with the photography as well as doing the lucid drawings which grace these pages. Howard Brainen and Karen Rogers of Custom Process Professional Photographic Laboratory made my sometimes very unprofessional exposures into beautiful prints. Amy Loughman contributed her talent, hard work, and financial support so generously that I can never repay her. This book would be very different without her, and rock climbing may be changed measurably because she has here demonstrated the art with such spirit and beauty.

Thank you.

Michael Loughman
January, 1981

Introduction

One of the chief attractions of climbing is the extraordinary richness of the possibilities. Children begin climbing on stairs and furniture, then quickly progress to playground apparatus, fences, trees, and small boulders. The possibilities are varied even for children. The greatest discovery of my early childhood was an old cannon in the town plaza. Later I spent countless hours climbing on the unfinished houses which sprouted everywhere on the hills above my home. In my high school years I discovered oil derricks, and then the sport called rock climbing. That was 1953.

Rock climbing has changed so much since the fifties that it is worth looking at the way it was then. My introduction was on a Sierra Club summer outing in the High Sierra. There were two hundred people on that trip, nearly all of whom were content to walk the trails and easy cross-country routes. However, a small, tightly knit, fanatical group raced up and down the 13,000-foot peaks. Back in camp they had exciting stories to tell. They seemed to inhabit a mysterious and more adventurous world of their own. So, intrigued, I climbed a few peaks. The climbs were fast and tiring and sometimes airy. Occasionally a rope was used, but the scariest times I remember were unroped: crossing steep snow slopes along the shores of lakes with broken sheets of ice floating on them.

That fall I joined the Sierra Club Rock Climbing Section in Los Angeles. The object of these climbers was not high, craggy summits but steep cracks and smooth faces on cliffs in the Southern California mountains. This kind of climbing was slow and demanding; sometimes climbers would spend a whole day struggling to gain ten feet on an unfinished route. This group included the best rock climbers in the country pioneering the most technically demanding routes, although scarcely anybody outside of the Southern California group had heard anything about this. A few years later I moved to Berkeley and joined the Sierra Club climbers there. Their technique was more primitive, but they were beginning to climb the "big walls" in Yosemite Valley.

In the fifties nearly all of the accomplished climbers in California belonged to the Sierra Club and a few college outing clubs. The situation was similar in other parts of the country; climbers were few, and they flocked together. It was necessary to go to the clubs to meet other climbers and learn what was happening. Learning to climb with a club was simple. You lived near one of the clubs and went on their regularly scheduled trips. If you didn't live near a climbing club, you probably had never heard of the esoteric sport.

In the sixties at least a few exceptional rock climbers appeared in every part of the country that had a reasonably accessible rock playground: New York, Washington, D. C., Wisconsin, Colorado, Utah, and the Northwest as well as California. At the same time, many of the best climbers, usually young, drifted away from organizations like the Sierra Club and the Appalachian Mountain Club. Even the college climbing clubs seemed to disintegrate. Climbing skills advanced, and climbing necessarily became a lifestyle for the leading climbers, who now were to be found in the climbing areas rather than in the cities where the organizations were based. Even those good climbers who went out only on weekends had little time for organizational activities. As the best climbers moved on, the clubs became poor places for the serious beginner to learn to climb.

In the seventies the tight little world of climbing exploded much as the world of skiing had exploded twenty years earlier. As part of the movement back to nature and physical fitness there appeared high school and college climbing courses, climbing magazines, climbing movies, and the ubiquitous mountain shops. In places like

Yosemite queues of climbers regularly formed at the base of the most popular routes. And along with the explosion of interest in climbing there has been a tendency toward specialization. Not only has rock climbing become a sport quite distinct from mountain climbing, but it has evolved into distinct varieties. We will consider some of these in Chapter 1.

Today rock climbing is a complex and highly sophisticated activity. Standards have advanced enormously, climbers are venturing onto ever more difficult terrain, and the gulf between the expert and the beginner has widened. Expert climbers are less willing to spend their precious climbing time with beginners. Promising beginners often start on what were the most difficult routes of twenty-five years ago. Learning to climb is no longer the straightforward matter it once was.

There are a few good specialized climbing schools; however, you cannot learn even the basics in one or two days or in the context of a class. You must learn on actual climbs in a one-to-one relation with a skilled climber. I will say more about schools and instruction in Chapter 2.

Rock-climbing courses are widely offered by clubs, colleges, and private instructors, but, unfortunately, much of this instruction is by people who are not skilled on hard rock. There are people who own a packful of gear and talk an impressive climb but avoid difficult terrain. Some like to instruct beginners and will even charge a fee. You must be prepared to make an independent evaluation of the instruction you receive; otherwise you may learn unrealistic or unsafe methods. You may be turned off by a wrong impression of the sport or a bad experience.

Rock climbing is full of beauty and grace. It is fun. And it is as safe as you wish to make it. Injuries and fatalities are commonplace, but they reflect the scarcity of competent instruction. Accidents are almost always the result of ignorance or carelessness. Here I must emphasize the difference between rock climbing and mountaineering. Big mountains are inherently dangerous, and mountain climbers usually must accept some exposure to avalanches and bad weather in order to get to the top. The list of expert mountaineers who have been killed climbing mountains is impressively long. Few of them made mistakes; they knew the risks, and eventually the odds caught up with them. In contrast, the list of expert rock climbers killed on rock cliffs is impressively short.

Probably most people teach themselves to climb; however, for the self-taught the road to climbing excellence is tortuous and full of unseen hazards. You will progress faster and more safely with expert companions. To find such companions, you must be highly motivated and do much for yourself.

This book is designed to help you bridge the difficult gap from beginning to a level of expertise that will get you into the circle of good climbers doing hard climbs. It will help you evaluate the quality of the instruction you receive. It is unique among climbing manuals in its emphasis on *free-climbing* technique, that is, on movement over the rock without the direct assistance of ropes and hardware. The rope and gear serve only as a safety net. *Aid climbing*, where the climbers hang from their equipment or use it to progress upward, and *big wall climbing*, which for all but the best climbers relies heavily on aid, are beyond the scope of this book. I believe that the beginner should master free climbing before going on to these pursuits.

The essence of climbing, as of dance, is creative movement. In the past the challenge of an imposing summit, the sheer technical difficulty of a route, or the adrenalin rush of acrobatics over thin air probably drew a certain type of person to climbing—and also limited its appeal. In the future, I believe, it will be the expressive, dancelike aspect of climbing that will broaden its appeal and offer the greatest scope for its development. I have tried to capture this quality in the photographs in this book. I hope that, better than words, they will convey to you the joys accessible to almost anyone close to level ground as well as high up on a big wall, close to the city as well as in the farthest range of the earth.

1

The Varieties of Climbing

The extraordinary richness of rock climbing, as it has evolved over the past thirty years, has made the sport accessible to people of all ages and nearly every physical condition, of varying personal goals and degrees of motivation, in every part of the country. Some will be satisfied climbing on a small boulder in a city park. Others will respond to the challenge of a multi-day climb on Yosemite's El Capitan. For others rock climbing is only a facet of a months-long expedition to Patagonia or the Karakoram.

Apart from geographical setting and inherent ease or difficulty, there are also very different methods of doing a climb. One climber will anchor his rope to the rock at six-foot intervals on a smooth wall, all the while scrupulously avoiding holding onto the anchors or rope to rest or help him up. They are intended only to catch a fall, but he is not likely to fall because he is as little willing to do that as to hang on the rope. His performance demands strength, technical mastery, and knowledge of himself. For another climber the same wall is at the limit of his ability. He places the same anchors at six-foot intervals, falls repeatedly, and rests on the rope. His performance demands less skill, but he is pushing his limits. He may ultimately push on to harder climbs than the first climber.

A third climber will aspire to do the same wall solo and without a rope. Probably he has climbed it already with a rope. Setting the anchors and rope in place takes strength and technical skill, so in one sense climbing without a rope is easier. However, the solo climber must have reserves of strength, exact self-knowledge, and unshakable self-discipline. A mistake or lapse of discipline could be fatal. He may wait months or years, carefully developing and assessing his skills, before he tries the climb. He may forgo this climb in favor of something easier.

The different approaches and goals of climbers have been called the games that climbers play. The most important variables in these games are *style* and *risk*. Let's look at these important concepts and then go on to the varieties of rock climbing.

Style and Risk

One of the constants in the history of climbing—perhaps the most conspicuous—is the pursuit of ever greater challenges. Once a summit has been reached, climbers look for a more difficult summit, then for a more difficult route to it. Once a route has been done, they try more exacting or "elegant" methods of doing it, usually involving self-imposed restrictions on equipment or techniques. For example, once Mount Everest was climbed with the help of oxygen, it became desirable or more elegant to climb it without oxygen. It is these self-imposed restrictions which constitute the *style* of a climb and which maintain the challenge in the face of advancing technology. The most elegant or stylish ascent is the one done without equipment (even, for some extremists, to the point of going nude and barefoot!). The climber should go alone, should go quickly and make the most extraordinary difficulties appear easy, and, ideally, should have no prior knowledge of the route.

The concern for style has played a major role in the evolution and advance of climbing. The sharp distinction between free climbing and aid climbing, for example, is a matter of style. It has not been made by all climbers in all places. Historically, many climbers have been ready to hold onto the rope whenever it proved convenient. El Capitan was first climbed in 1958 with extensive aid, and until recently it would have been unthinkable without aid. Other climbers have eschewed aid even to the point of failing repeatedly on a hard climb. It is the ready and willing aid climbers who have pioneered the more impressive rock walls, such as El Capitan. However, the people who insist on the sharp distinction between free ascents and aided ascents have often become the better climbers. Today several El Cap routes have been climbed free or nearly free.

A climb need not be difficult in order to be done stylishly. At least a few climbers would rather do an elegant job on an easy route than simply get up a hard one.

Another constant in the history of climbing is risk, especially the risk of falling. The first and third climbers in the example at the beginning of this chapter have both climbed in what is today judged good style; however, the solo climber has exposed himself to the possibility of a serious fall. Though climbers have sought out risk, for obvious reasons they have tried to control it. Historically, they have not placed great faith in the rope. The risk of falling has been controlled chiefly by adopting a particular stance on the slope, always keeping three points of contact with it, and proceeding in a slow and deliberate manner. The climber pauses at some resting point, studies the terrain, plans the next moves, perhaps moves forward just enough to test them, rests again, and then executes the moves to the next rest.

But climbers are tackling ever smoother and steeper terrain. Rests may be few and far between. On an exceedingly smooth slope the climber may rely on momentum. He may leap for a hold. On steep or overhanging terrain he may rely on speed, hoping to get to a distant resting point before his strength fails. In any case, strength and speed are to some extent interchangeable. It is a matter of elementary physics. Force (or strength) is necessary to set a body in motion, but bodies in motion tend to stay in motion. Often the trick in a very difficult move is to make it quickly. Climbing is becoming more dynamic. Climbing has always been a kind of dance, but it is becoming allegro instead of adagio.

The requirement of speed suggests a new kind of training (see Talus Running). The climber must learn to see terrain and respond to it quickly, with a minimum of thought between the seeing and the doing. He must climb more automatically, more by conditioning than by deliberation.

Peak Bagging

For many people the object of climbing is the summit. It can be an easy summit by the easiest route. "Peak baggers" often have little knowledge of climbing techniques and scarcely think of themselves as climbers. The summit offers a view and a fixed point for turning around. Beyond the view, the exercise, and the companionship of the ascent, peak baggers may ask no more. Some do like to go quickly and "collect" as many summits as possible.

Among climbers the term *peak bagger* can be a pejorative, perhaps because the activity requires no unusual skills, and the elements of challenge and risk are less conspicuous. However, for the beginner peak bagging can be both instructive and stylish. And it is readily accessible. Beyond the usual requirements of high-elevation backpacking no special equipment or technical knowledge is needed to reach most mountain summits in the United States. The beginner need only go to a high elevation in nearby mountains, look around for an easy summit, and go to it. The chief hazards are knocking rocks loose, slipping on steep snow, and bad weather; nothing more than ordinary prudence is necessary to avoid these hazards. Of course, the inexperienced mountaineer may well go with a companion or two.

Peak bagging is an excellent way to strengthen your legs and build overall stamina and body condition. Backpacking will do the same, but I would rather climb a peak than carry a pack. Much high-mountain terrain consists of talus slopes, and these provide the opportunity for a valuable exercise described in the next section—talus running. As for style, the peak bagger needs no special gear. You can go quickly. You can go alone. You can make light of the difficulties, which are likely to be modest. You need not follow a map or guidebook, nor even reach the summit. You can simply concentrate on fluid and beautiful movement.

Running talus. *Photo by Bruce Robinson.*

Talus Running

So far *talus running* has relatively few adherents. However, it has been recognized as extraordinary training for rock climbing, especially for the new more dynamic mode of climbing.

The best talus for the beginner is nearly level and consists of blocks about three feet across. Just walking on talus takes some getting used to. You must learn how well your feet will stick on the ever-changing angles of surfaces, how to move your body smoothly from one balance point to the next, how to cope with the occasional shifting of blocks under you. As you gain confidence, you can increase your speed. Because for the beginner talus running takes intense concentration, your nervous system may fatigue quickly, and you will need frequent rests. It is exactly this concentration which practice reduces to a minimum. After awhile the countless little responses come easily. Body and mind are finely tuned.

When you are ready, you can move onto steeper slopes and larger blocks. On the largest blocks the hands come into play, but the talus runner continues to lope along more like a monkey than the traditional slow-paced image of a mountain climber. Like a dancer, the talus runner has endless opportunities for creative or stylish movement: graceful leaps, delicate balances, and intricate series of leaps and balances. Yet in some ways the art is more interesting than dance. The terrain is an ever-changing stage, and the next demands of it are not completely known. The talus runner has a theme but must improvise upon it quickly.

Falls on talus can be serious. If you start to fall, keep your feet out of the holes between blocks. Cushion your body with your hands, but relax your body. I have collapsed in a heap many times on talus and have as yet escaped injury. Be alert also to the fact that some kinds of rock have especially sharp edges. Granite is relatively safe, but falls on fine-textured metamorphic or volcanic rocks easily produce nasty cuts.

Neither heavy mountain boots nor rock-climbing shoes are well suited to talus running. Stiff-soled boots provide poor friction and impede the springing action of the feet. Shoes properly fitted for rock climbing are too tight for talus running. Jogging or cross-country shoes are best. These should have thick but flexible soles that will protect the feet from bruises. Other than that, bruises are avoided by stepping lightly. Remember the monkey, the dancer, and the cat. They are your models.

Bouldering

Bouldering is rock climbing close to ground level, where an unchecked fall is not necessarily serious. The boulderer uses no rope or specialized gear except climbing shoes and gymnastic chalk (used to keep the hands dry) and needs no companions. Imagination and a tiny bit of cliff are all that is required. If the cliff is close to home or work, a few minutes a day are sufficient for this exercise.

Bouldering has played a major role in the advance of climbing standards. Often the boulderer operates only a few feet or even a few inches above gentle ground, and if a fall is inconsequential, he may push himself to the limit of his ability and make repeated efforts until he finally masters an extremely difficult and complex problem. Often several boulderers will work together on a problem, combining their inventive powers and indulging in a friendly competition until the problem is solved.

A very small cliff may appear to offer limited scope for climbing, but if the routes are too easy or routine, the inventive boulderer may put certain holds "off route" or restrict himself to a prescribed set of holds. He may do the problems with only one hand, with no hands or with no feet, or with one hand and one foot. Perhaps he will simply concentrate on a fluid and beautiful style. If the cliff is too low for sustained climbs upward, he can climb sideways.

All of these exercises are valuable training for longer climbs, but bouldering is more than preparation for other climbing; it is a recreation and art complete in itself. It is here that the climber is freest to be creative and to invent moves that are not required by the terrain.

A climber and belayer using a top rope.

Top Roping

When bouldering, you may venture high enough above a safe landing that a fall would be serious. At some point, because of the difficulty or the length of a fall, you will want the protection of a climbing rope.

Any method that will check a falling climber by means of a rope is called a *belay* (see Chapter 4). The simplest involves a companion, the *belayer*, who assumes a braced or anchored stance above the climber, holds the rope that is tied to the climber, and takes in the slack rope. Alternatively, the belayer may be stationed at the base of the route. The rope then runs up to a pulleylike anchor point and back down to the climber. If the belay stance or anchor is directly above the climber, any fall will be short. Thus the climber may proceed with perfect security and, as in bouldering, he may push himself to the limit.

If the top of the cliff is reached and the belay set up by means of an easy, alternate route which does not require the protection of the rope, then the climbing is called *top roping*. It provides a quick and secure way for the climber to develop technique and stamina on longer, more sustained pitches of rock. However, the danger of top roping is that the climber may become dependent on the security of a top rope.

Leader and belayer on a fifth-class climb.

Fifth Class Climbing

Often there is no easy way round to a belay stance or anchor above the climber. Someone must climb up first. If the leader climbs without the protection of a rope, he is climbing *third class* (see Chapter 6 for a complete definition of classes of climbing). If the rope simply trails down behind the leader to a belayer stationed below, he is climbing *fourth class*. Obviously, as the leader climbs higher above the belayer, there is less and less practical difference between fourth class and third class. At some point, perhaps only five or ten feet above the belayer, a fall will become very serious. In fourth class climbing the rope serves mainly to protect the second climber, who has, in effect, a top rope.

As the leader proceeds, he may shorten the length of a possible fall by anchoring his rope to the rock at points along the way. The rope slides freely through a *carabiner* (a metal link with a gate for admitting the rope) attached to the anchor. Then if he falls ten feet above his last anchor or *protection*, he will drop twenty feet before the rope begins to check him. This mode of climbing, with intermediate protection points between the leader and the belayer, is called *fifth class*.

On steep rock with modern equipment and methods, falls of twenty and even forty feet do not usually cause serious injury. The steeper and smoother the rock, the less likely the falling climber is to scrape or bounce against it before the rope checks him. Thus difficult terrain is often inherently safer than easy terrain. While the layman associates the greatest hazard with vertical or overhanging rock, climbers know that a fall through space to a soft landing against the end of the resilient climbing rope is relatively safe.

In twenty-seven years of rock climbing I have taken four falls longer than twenty-five feet. These falls resulted in one scraped elbow and one sprained ankle. I believe my experience is testi-

mony to the efficiency of modern equipment and methods. Of course, the climber must know when it is reasonable to proceed to the point of a fall.

The varieties of climbing described so far are all free climbing, that is, the climber moves over the rock using only the holds the rock itself provides. He does not hold onto a rope or other gear except to place it in position to check a possible fall. He does not even lean against the rope or an anchor to rest. The rope and gear are a safety net. They serve only as protection against the worst consequences of a fall.

Aid Climbing

Where the rock does not offer adequate holds, the climber may attach a variety of devices to the rock for aid points. The climbing is then *aid climbing* (formerly called *sixth class*).

Aid may be employed to make a route easier than it would be as a free climb, or to extend the possible worlds the climber can explore. It may require a high level of mechanical imagination and skill in addition to the same physical skills and mental control involved in free climbing. A mixture of aided moves and free moves can be especially demanding.

Although some routes are inconceivable without aid, there is a very impressive tradition of aid climbs eventually "going free." The two varieties of climbing offer different experiences, but the prevalent feeling among climbers is that free climbing is the more elegant mode. Thus the first free ascent of an aid route generally attracts recognition and approval from the climbing community, while an aided ascent of a route which has gone free does not.

As I mentioned in the Introduction, the specialized techniques for aid climbing are beyond the scope of this book.

Big Wall Climbing

Routes of such length and sustained difficulty that climbers usually spend several days on them are *big walls*. The most famous big wall routes are those on El Capitan in Yosemite Valley. The climbing ordinarily involves hauling heavy loads of gear, much aid climbing, and much mounting of fixed ropes by means of mechanical ascenders (*jumaring*). On big walls style is usually subordinated to the objective of getting to the top.

Big walls offer grand adventure and make great demands on the climbers' skill and tenacity, but I must here admit to certain prejudices. I have an especial dislike for hauling and jumaring. They are too much like work, and jumaring is really scary. And I don't care for aid climbing. So I am not a wall climber. I do have a couple of comments to offer as something of an outside observer.

First, I am always amazed to see eager, inexpert climbers tackle big walls. They surround themselves with piles of sophisticated gear, spend hours poring over it, then inch slowly up the wall. All too often they think that in a few days on El Cap they have reached the pinnacle of climbing accomplishment, never realizing how much they have relied on equipment. Over the years since the first big wall climbs, improvements in equipment have made pitches which were once near the limit of the possible into relatively straightforward mechanical operations. Of course, expert climbers have maintained the challenge of big walls by free climbing many former aid pitches or by moving on to new and more difficult aid problems. All too often, however, beginners who are drawn to big walls focus on the application of sophisticated gear rather than on the development of climbing skills.

Second, a well-developed sense of style seems to me especially important to the preservation of wall-climbing values, but more about that later (Chapters 4 and 6).

Free Soloing

One September day in 1976, at the Shawangunks in New York State, I was leading 150 feet above the ground, clipping my rope into the fixed protection, when an elderly gentleman climbed past me a few feet to one side. He was doing an easier route, but like all Shawangunks routes, it was practically vertical. He climbed alone with no rope or gear except a few runners and carabiners slung over his shoulder. We traded greetings, and I watched him struggle with a strenuous move. It was not difficult to guess that I was watching Fritz Wiessner. He was one of the leading climbers in Europe in the 1920s; fifty years later he was free soloing Three Pines at the "Gunks." Three Pines is a "beginner's climb," but I thought, There is something to which I aspire: a certain longevity and a purity of style which imply much.

Free soloing is not for beginners, as it demands exacting study. The free soloer who expects to live very long will approach the rock rather more cautiously and carefully than his colleague with a belay. He will not push his limits. He will not attempt some routes, such as face climbs on especially tiny holds, because they are less forgiving of misjudgments. He will move more slowly and deliberately, relying on great physical and mental reserves. And he will have made a thorough study of the art of climbing down.

Most expert climbers go alone and unroped on difficult terrain at least occasionally. Free soloing seems either the craziest thing a climber can do or else the ultimate accomplishment. If climbing is viewed as the exploration of one's inner resources, rather than as the conquest of a wall, then certainly free soloing is the ultimate step. I have noticed this about it: Rarely has an expert climber been killed free soloing a difficult route. And never have I met a free soloer who seemed anything but humbled by the experience.

Buildering

It should be no surprise that climbers are sometimes unable to resist the opportunities afforded by a building. Or that frustrated climbers turn to buildings when rock is not handy. On university campuses especially climbers have employed ropes and the full range of climbing techniques to scale buildings. This is usually done at night and commonly gets the climbers into trouble. Once I was minding my own business on a second-story window ledge when a policeman accosted me with, "What are you doing up there?"

I responded impulsively, "I'm a burglar." He did not have the grace to laugh.

Much trouble can be saved by restricting oneself to daytime or evening *buildering*—what is, in effect, low-level bouldering on artificial structures. It is best to go without gear and to have a story ready, such as: "I tossed my cap in the air, and it landed up there."

The San Francisco Bay Area rock outcrops close to my home do not afford many opportunities for crack climbing, which employs a set of techniques distinct from those used to climb smooth or steep faces. However, good cracks are common on buildings, especially where two buildings come close together without quite touching. A fifteen-minute walk from my home through downtown Berkeley takes me past four excellent cracks and several other interesting problems.

Buildering is both practice for rock climbing and an art in itself. Problems are less obvious than those on rock, and the techniques required to solve them may be bizarre.

It is to be hoped that one day authorities will recognize that buildings are a vast and legitimate resource for recreation, especially in the inner cities. However, that recognition will require a profound social revolution.

2

Getting Started

Many beginners seem to think that the ability to rock climb, like the ability to fly, is a native endowment: Birds fly; people cannot. Some people climb well; others cannot. The first thing you should know about climbing is that it is a learned art.

Over the years I have watched many beginners become good climbers. Some had obvious talent at the start: an already developed strength and agility, an aggressive approach to the problems offered by the rock, perhaps a willingness to risk a tumble. Others seemed very unlikely climbers: "unathletic," overweight, flabby, clumsy, afraid of heights, over forty. One of the two or three most brilliant American climbers of the 1950s, Mark Powell, was described by an early climbing companion as "awkward as a cow." I have known a very capable climber with one leg and another who is totally blind. Both did their share of the leading on climbs. I have concluded that almost anyone can learn to climb well. It does require motivation and hard work. Usually, it also requires skilled companions.

There are pitfalls which confront the beginner. Many beginners have been turned away from climbing by a false sense of inferiority, by the wrong companions or incompetent instruction, even by the lack of proper climbing shoes. In this chapter I will try to guide you around the pits and into the course where you will make the most rapid progress.

Women Climbers

Climbing is still male dominated, and sexism is rampant. There are still relatively few good women climbers to serve as models, and women need models of their own sex, partly to demonstrate that "male" strength is not needed to do hard climbs. Women tend to think that difficult climbing, on overhangs, for example, takes a kind of strength in the shoulders and arms they don't have. By now most experienced climbers know better; women have done many of the climbs supposed to be especially strenuous.

On the average, women are not as strong as men in an absolute sense, but they also are not as heavy so they don't need as much strength. On the average, smaller people have a better strength-to-weight ratio, which is what counts in climbing. In any case, strength can be developed.

The main physical handicap women have is not in strength, but in height. When a handhold is out of reach, a short person must be a better climber than someone who can reach that hold. At Berkeley's Indian Rock several five-foot-four climbers and one five-foot-one woman have done many of the hard problems on which height is a definite advantage, but they must employ both greater strength and greater skill on these problems than taller climbers. Fortunately, most rock does not favor tall people as much as Indian Rock does. There are situations where small people have the advantage—for example, thin cracks which will admit only the smallest fingers.

Women may also be hindered by lack of strong motivation and confidence. The best climbers have a powerful drive to climb, as if they cannot keep away from the rock. This kind of drive seems to be rarer in women than in men, probably because the expectation of success is an important element in it. At the start women must believe that they can learn to climb well. At the highest levels of accomplishment women must believe that they can climb as well as any man.

Couples and Children

Conspicuously few couples climb together successfully. There are probably obscure psychological reasons for this, having to do with ego and insecurity. More obviously, spouses and lovers develop sensitivities to each other which can be detrimental to a successful climbing relationship.

A second on a fifth-class climb.

Hard climbing demands a level of detachment. Further, it is improbable that a couple will be well-matched in their goals and abilities. Rather than delve into this difficult area, I simply offer the following advice: (1) Don't learn to climb from your lover or spouse. (2) Don't expect to do most of your climbing with him or her.

Similar problems and the same advice apply to parents and children. I am particularly incensed to see a reluctant child pushed by an overzealous parent. Father: "You can do it." Child: "No, I can't." This dialogue is followed by tears, anger, and resentment; the child is turned off. Some of these parents even appear to be otherwise intelligent and sensitive people who should know better. To paraphrase an old saw: You can lead a child to the rock, but you cannot make the child enjoy climbing.

Climbing as adults know it, like driving a car, is an adult activity. It must be entirely restructured before young children are likely to do well at it. I doubt that many adults know how to do this restructuring; probably it would involve starting on a special apparatus rather than on rocks. If you want to climb with your child, you had best be guided by his sense of how to do it. Avoid giving too many directions. Let the child learn mainly by watching others.

Teenage Climbers

When teenagers take an interest in climbing, most parents are beset by dread of possible consequences. People have been killed climbing. Teenagers have been known to chuck a dull school routine for the excitement, challenge, and status offered by climbing. They have even left home for the fabled freedom of the hills.

From one viewpoint climbing is a frivolous and dangerous activity. From another it is a rich and rewarding lifestyle. In the sixties I went to a university when many of my climbing companions went to Yosemite. Then I taught for five years. I learned two things: My love for climbing was too important to be sacrificed that way, and most high school graduates are not ready to plod through four to ten more years of school. As a teacher, I met countless young people who were putting in their time in college because they didn't have the imagination or drive to do anything else. Climbing is a rich and demanding activity. If I had a son or daughter who preferred it even to the exclusion of more conventional pursuits, I certainly would not worry about it.

The physical hazards of climbing are a more difficult problem for parents (see Chapter 6 for a discussion of climbing safety). Few parents have the knowledge to judge the safeness of their children's climbing or the inclination to participate. And in most cases parents aren't wanted. So what are concerned parents to do? Since the safest way to climb is with expert companions, parents can encourage a teenager to seek out expert climbers and learn from them. These are most likely to be found in either popular bouldering sites such as Berkeley's Indian Rock or major climbing areas such as Yosemite Valley or the Shawangunks in New York State. Parents can make sure the teenager has access to these important sites. Instruction at a reputable climbing school in one of the major areas is also helpful. However, one or two days of instruction do not equip a person to proceed alone; expert companions are still necessary.

Clubs, Courses, and Schools

Clubs played a major role in the early development of rock climbing. Today, however, few serious climbers have the time or taste for organizational activities. The clubs do attract more than their share of beginners with only a passing interest in climbing. A great deal of time is spent instructing beginners in the most elementary aspects of belaying, rappelling, and prusiking in "practice rock" situations which bear little relation to climbing realities. Many people never progress beyond the beginning level. Perhaps that was their intention, but I suspect that the club did not provide the opportunity or stimulus.

If you don't have climbing friends and cannot afford a climbing school, then a club may have something to offer. Usually there are a few experienced climbers who can teach you the basics in a realistic manner, but you must seek them out.

Rock-climbing courses offered by clubs, high schools, colleges, and private instructors must always be approached with caution. In the United States anyone can set up in business as a climbing instructor or guide. Some are incompetent; for example, I have seen paid instructors who carefully avoided moving over the rock for fear of undermining the confidence of their clients. Nevertheless, the climbing community has steadfastly resisted efforts to establish licensing or regulation for climbing professionals. A *laissez-faire* spirit has been a peculiarity of the American climbing tradition.

In my observation high school climbing courses are the worst places to learn to climb. The courses are superficial and often focused on rappelling, and the teachers are seldom expert climbers. Rappelling is the *last* thing that should be taught in the high school context (see Chapter 5). College climbing courses are usually better because colleges tend to hire competent instructors. However, colleges can make mistakes, and there is no real monitoring of college climbing courses.

The few good specialized climbing schools that exist are located in the climbing areas rather than in cities. You should inquire locally for recommendations. If a climbing school is well known to local climbers, then it is likely to offer competent, even excellent instruction. There are two reasons for this: First, good climbers in the area are likely to work for the school. Second, they would not tolerate incompetence; they would make it the butt of jokes.

What a climbing school can do for you is limited or else expensive. As I have noted before, you cannot learn even the basics in one or two days or in the context of a class; you must learn on actual climbs in a one-to-one relation with your mentor. If you learn with an expert professional, expect to spend several hundred dollars for the basic instruction.

Clubs, courses, and schools all focus on teaching the use of climbing ropes and gear. That is what would-be climbers expect, and it is easier to teach than the more sophisticated, physically demanding movement skills. But what the serious beginner needs most is exposure to climbers skilled in moving over the rock.

Where to Start and Who to Look For

If you don't have a friend who is a climber, go to the local mountain shop. Ask to talk to an experienced climber. Ask about the bouldering or top-roping site most favored by the local climbers. If there isn't any, ask about the nearest major climbing area; it will have bouldering, too. Don't buy anything!

Spring and fall are the busiest seasons at most bouldering sites, as climbers tend to go off to distant places during the summer. Set aside a Saturday or Sunday for climber watching and take yourself to the rock. Go in the afternoon and plan to stay until dark. Many climbers get up late and start slow. In any case, bouldering tends to be an end-of-the-day activity. It is good bouldering that you want to see at the start. Unless you are at an especially popular site, you may have to come back several times.

When you see good bouldering, you will know at once: It is breathtaking. It may also be discouraging. The expert boulderer will move quickly and gracefully on terrain you cannot climb at all. That is the minimum level of skill you should look for. When a beginner, even a talented one, finds himself able to do climbs which are difficult for his instructor, that is a sure sign that he is not with a skilled climber.

Many climbers will object to my emphasis on bouldering skill. It is true that many good climbers do not care for bouldering and that some skilled boulderers do not do fifth class climbing. However, my premise is that movement is the essence of climbing, and the beginner should attain some skill at it before becoming involved with equipment. I believe you should know what skilled movement looks like right at the start. You can evaluate bouldering skills more easily than other climbing skills. Clumsy, inept bouldering is pretty obvious, whereas the dangerous belay or rappel is not always apparent. Furthermore, I have never met a skilled boulderer who didn't have a sound grasp of the use of equipment. Skilled bouldering and skilled fifth class climbing demand the same quality of intellectual discipline.

Even the most skilled boulderer will struggle and perhaps even fall repeatedly on a problem of exceptional difficulty. However, a thoughtful approach, controlled movements, and a tenacious grip on the rock are generally signs of competence; beware of the climber who seems to pop off the rock easily.

Above all, don't be put off by the sight of climbing excellence. Some climbers may be more talented than others, but climbing skill is not a gift bestowed on the chosen few; it is a learned art. It is mainly a process of discovering what your body can do. With proper guidance any beginner can do climbs far beyond what seemed possible on the very first day. After that, progress requires dedication and hard work. If you sometimes become frustrated or discouraged, you are making progress.

It is very easy, as a beginner, to watch expert climbers, then try a few tough problems for yourself and conclude that you haven't some necessary capacity. You cannot even get off the ground on something that looked easy when someone else did it. You should bear firmly in mind that climbers have been exploring particular sites for many years, always seeking greater challenges. Some climbers devote most of their time to conditioning their bodies and mastering outrageously difficult problems. They may have done a particular problem a hundred times and got it "wired" so that it *is* ridiculously easy for them. They may work for hours or days or months on a problem and then spring it on someone else as if that person should be able to do it right off. This is known as *sandbagging*. Locals love to sandbag visiting experts from other areas. Beginners may be sandbagged inadvertently by an expert who says something is "easy." Just remember that it is considered stylish to make light of difficulties.

Who to Look Out For

Now here is a touchy subject. I spend a lot of time at popular climbing sites, and almost every time I go to one, I am shocked by some display of ignorance or misguidance. All too often these demonstrations lead to accidents which involve everyone on the scene. Over twenty-seven years I have helped carry out eleven broken climbers. Two of them were dead. None was what I would call a skilled climber. Of course, accidents happen to some of the best climbers, too, but considering the number and severity of hard climbs in the United States, the safety record of skilled climbers is astoundingly good.

The rocks attract all too many people who own a packful of gear, talk an impressive climb, but avoid difficult terrain. Many of these climbers simply have not learned how to move over the rock. Instead, they focus on the use of ropes and gear, and sometimes struggle up climbs by means far different from the norm. Unfortunately, their attitude makes it unlikely that they will master even these skills. At some point they are likely to overstep their limited skills and hurt themselves or endanger others. Recently, one such adventurer decided he had undertaken a route beyond his abilities, so he crossed above me onto the easy route I was doing. I was forty feet above my last anchor. While I hurriedly placed another anchor and cringed against the rock, I watched him make an exhausted bellyflop onto a ledge just above me.

What I am talking about here is the major hazard in climbing: the supposition that equipment and procedures with equipment can serve as a substitute for skill in moving over the rock. In fact, most of the people who focus on equipment don't understand it very well because they have not used it on hard rock. They understand neither the limitations of equipment nor the nuances of its use.

If you have the misfortune to fall into the hands of someone who fits this profile, you may be turned off; waste a lot of time; or learn things about equipment, belays, and rappels you are better off not knowing. As a rule of thumb in seeking good climbing companions and instruction, beware of people who do two or more of the following:

1. Carry large amounts of rope and hardware to bouldering and top-roping sites.

2. Talk mostly about equipment and procedures with equipment (i.e., belaying, rappelling, prusiking, jumaring). Of course, an instructor must talk about these things, but ask for a demonstration of skilled movement on the rock.

3. Talk about their climbing experiences in the military. Military objectives and methods bear little relation to civilian practice.

4. Throw a good rope down in the dirt.

5. Rock climb in heavy mountain boots. Expert mountaineers will occasionally do this, but they are easy to spot, as they move over difficult rock very easily.

6. Spend a lot of time rappelling. Expert climbers hate to rappel; it is the most dangerous thing they have to do.

Climbing Shoes

If what you see on your first day at the rock intrigues you, come back soon with a pair of climbing shoes. Of course, you can climb without them—some of the best climbers do climbs of extreme difficulty barefooted—but for the beginner proper shoes make an enormous difference. It is sad to see a promising beginner frustrated by bad shoes, usually not even aware that the shoes are the cause of the difficulty. Good shoes will reveal undreamed-of possibilities.

Mountain boots are not good shoes for rock climbing. They are designed for cold weather and for cramponing on steep ice. It takes some skill to use them successfully on difficult rock. You probably are better off barefooted than trying to rock climb in mountain boots. Rock-climbing shoes are light and flexible. They resemble tennis shoes except that they have smooth black rubber soles. They do not have cleats or lugs like many hiking or mountain boots. They are immorally expensive. At the start borrow a pair if you can, even for a few hours. Otherwise, break down and buy them. If after a few times you lose interest in climbing, you can easily resell the shoes for ten dollars off the new price. You will have invested ten dollars in finding out what climbing is really like.

For many years the great bulk of hard rock climbing in this country has been done in the French-made shoes called EB's. EB's have been so popular because they work incredibly well. In the beginning at least they will outperform your head. They will stick when you expect them to slip. It takes some time to learn to use them to their full potential.

However, there are many problems with EB's. Climbers like snug shoes, but snug EB's can become extremely painful, so you may find yourself loosening or even removing your shoes at belay stances. Over several years of climbing EB's can cause damage to the structure of your feet. Beware of getting them too small.

EB's have always worn out quickly, and in recent years, despite great increases in price, they have become even more fragile. However, if you learn to place your feet on holds carefully, you can easily get twice as much wear out of your shoes as a climber with sloppy footwork. You can also make modifications in your shoes which will extend their life. Leather can be glued (contact cement) and/or stitched over the canvas portions of the uppers. Holes that wear in the rubber can be patched with plastic rubber, but it must be applied frequently. EB's are difficult to resole successfully, but several shops in this country specialize in this work and accept mail orders. Experienced climbers can direct you to them.

Several manufacturers are now producing shoes which are close copies of EB's. So far these shoes do not perform as well as EB's, but some of them are cheaper, more comfortable, and more durable. They may be worth it. Don't accept the recommendation of salespeople in a mountain

Figure 1. Edging with a mountain boot.

shop. Inquire of the most skilled climbers you can find at the rock.

When I started climbing, no one had specialized rock shoes. Climbers used either mountain boots or tennis shoes. Mountain boots were used as what we now call *edging* shoes **(Figure 1).** They were preferred where the footholds were more or less tiny but well-defined ledges. The rigid edge of a boot sole would catch on remarkably small ledges; a ledge 1/8-inch wide suffices. However, stiff boot soles did not conform to slopes where purchase depends on friction between the sole and the rock. Nor did boots permit free flexure of the feet and ankles. Indeed, the climber who did not hold his boot still in the required position might suddenly pop off one of those tiny ledges.

Tennis shoe edges bend and slide off tiny ledges, but the soles conform to slopes. Tennis shoes were used as *smearing* shoes **(Figure 2).** The climber placed the ball of the foot on the slope, perhaps covering or "smearing" the vicinity of a tiny ledge. He relied on the soft rubber adhering to the rock by deformation and friction.

Today's rock-climbing shoes are a compromise between boots and tennis shoes. EB's have relatively flexible soles of soft rubber that make them especially effective for smearing. Many climbers learn to do hard edging in them, but this certainly places more strain on the feet than edg-

ing with stiffer shoes. The EB climber probably develops stronger feet. Practically every serious climber owns a pair of EB's, but many also acquire other kinds of shoes for specific reasons—for example, shoes that are more durable, more easily resoled, more comfortable, or better for edging. Some other shoes are especially suited for bouldering or for aid climbing. Most of these other shoes come with a hard rubber sole; they perform better when it is replaced with a softer sole, either "green plug" Neoprene or Nitrene. Many climbers are learning to resole their own shoes as shoe repairs are costly and, unless the cobblers happen to be climbers, they generally do not trim a sole properly for climbing.

Having warned you not to buy shoes that are too small, I must now caution you not to get them too large. Your shoes should conform to your feet the way good gloves fit your hands. In particular, your toes should reach to the tip of the shoe. If there is any space at the end of your toes, you will not be able to "toe in" to the rock effectively (see Chapter 3, Using Your Feet). With EB's I recommend finding the smallest size that will accept your foot without doubling up the toes or arch (it will not be comfortable), then buying one size larger (not particularly comfortable, either).

Properly fit climbing shoes are not comfortable for walking. Climbers routinely carry a second pair of shoes for the hike down after a climb.

Figure 2. Smearing with a rock-climbing shoe.

First Steps

When you have located the favorite local bouldering or top roping site and equipped yourself with climbing shoes, you are ready to proceed farther. Let me emphasize again that your progress will be safest, surest, and most rapid with expert companions. In my experience these climbers are usually ready to help even an unknown beginner at a bouldering or top roping site, but are, of course, less ready to take the beginner on longer, fifth class climbs. However, once you have mastered the basic skills, especially skill in moving over the rock, you will have no trouble finding expert companions for longer climbs.

Over many years of experience with beginning climbers I have found a sequence of steps in the learning process which works very well. This sequence is outlined below and provides the basic organization for the chapters which follow.

1. *Movement.* When beginners are taught "climbing," they are customarily taught about ropes, tie-ins, anchors, belays, rappels, and the like at a top-roping site; the techniques of movement they usually must discover for themselves by the slow and uncertain method of trial and error. However, since movement is the essence of climbing, I think you should attain some skill at it before you learn to tie into a rope. You can do this close to level ground at a bouldering site. Without a rope you will focus on the rock itself and on your own body, spending the maximum time actually moving over the rock. Thus in this book I will reverse the customary order of things and start with movement in Chapter 3.

By starting without a rope, you will learn also the essential principle of climbing safety: Safety depends on your ability to stand on the rock correctly, to judge the terrain ahead and the consequences of a fall, and sometimes to climb down from a hard place.

Many unskilled climbers want to get up the hardest place they can manage with a struggle. Of course, you will need to struggle on hard climbs to become a skilled climber, and you will probably want the protection of a rope if you are more than five or ten feet above the deck. In the beginning, however, I think you should concentrate on technique, control, and a smooth, fluid style. Difficult moves can be mastered within a few feet of the ground. You can venture higher up, where a fall would be serious, without a rope so long as you are on relatively easy terrain and are practicing the discipline of climbing; that is, the judgment, the control, and the readiness to climb down.

Sometimes you will slip from a hard place or need to "bail out," so you must be prepared. Having decided in advance that the risk of a fall is reasonable, you will have selected a level landing place. If you land on a slope or a protruding stone, you are likely to hurt an ankle. If you fall from an awkward position, you may strike your head or injure your back. Boulderers often "spot" each other closely and carefully to prevent a bad landing.

2. *Anchors and belays.* You can learn the rudiments of anchors and belays in the context of top roping on a small cliff. However, full competence in these crucial skills is attained only on longer climbs under the tutelage of an experienced leader. I will consider the general principles and the basic procedures of protection with the climbing rope and anchors in Chapter 4.

3. *Rappels and prusiks.* In the unlikely event that your experienced leader makes a disastrous error or gets hit by a falling rock, you should be prepared to get yourself off the cliff. So before you venture onto longer climbs (as opposed to bouldering and top roping) you should learn to rappel, to rig and retrieve the rappel rope, and to prusik. These procedures are treated in Chapter 5.

4. *Leading.* I believe you should start leading as soon as you have mastered the basic skills, preferably during your first day of fifth class climbing. Thus you can make a natural and quick transition from boulderer without a rope to leader at the "sharp end" of the rope. However, you should make your first leads with the guidance of a thoroughly experienced climber. Leading and related matters are discussed in Chapter 6.

3

Movement

Learning how to move over rock is largely a matter of learning to use your feet, to keep in balance over them, and to rely as little as possible on your arms and hands. In this chapter we will begin with feet and balance climbing, then progress to more strenuous and sophisticated techniques and to the specialized techniques for climbing cracks.

Climbing is done primarily with the legs and feet because they are far stronger than arms and hands. We can stand on our feet for hours at a time but hang from our arms for a few minutes at best. Thus the most essential element of climbing technique is *balance*. The object is to keep your body poised directly over your point of support (i.e., foothold) like a top or a ballerina on pointe. Movement then becomes a matter of making a neat transition from one point of support to the next.

Climbers often deliberately make movements that are out of balance. That is, they lean against their arms. This is done because it is necessary—as we will see in some of the techniques discussed later in this chapter—but it uses up precious strength. Ideally, the climber gets back into balance as quickly as possible, so that he can rest his arms and hands.

The best place to learn footwork and balance climbing is a "beginner's slope," that is, a relatively smooth, low-angle slope, perhaps of only 45 or 50 degrees. A good beginner's slope is not necessarily easy. It lacks good handholds and demands that you stand on your feet. One or two days spent mastering such a slope will pay large dividends later on. Mastering a beginner's slope means climbing it repeatedly until you are completely at ease on it. You should then climb down

it and try climbing it with one hand, and then with no hands. These excellent exercises literally force you to use your feet well and to move your body correctly.

Good footwork and correct body movements are particularly important for women, who usually have less power in their arms and shoulders than men. However, even very powerful men will quickly find that they can't rely on strength to get them up most climbs. This was impressed upon me during one of my first days on the rock in the early 1950s. A gentleman from Santa Monica's Muscle Beach, a former Mr. America, showed up at a Sierra Club local climb. He took off his shirt, pumped up his muscles, and acted as if he would take the climbing world by storm. He was shown a smooth, low-angle slab of granite where his biceps were useless. He couldn't climb it. Wasn't there something with handholds? He was shown the local Beginner's Crack, which was not difficult but would surely sandbag most beginners. It had large "bucket" holds, but overhung slightly. He tried to haul himself up with his arms, but he wasn't quick and clever enough with his hands. When he had given up, a slender sixteen-year-old girl tied into the rope and "walked" easily up the overhang. Mr. America put on his shirt and never came back. When I am having trouble on a climb, I often think of him and tell myself, "You got to use your feet."

Using Your Feet

The natural tendency of beginners is to look up for handholds. You must begin your education as a climber by learning to *look down for footholds*. In the beginning keep your hands down below your shoulders and tell yourself repeatedly: *look down; look down!*

Once you have the habit of looking down, you must learn to see footholds. They may be very small or steeply sloping (see **Figure 7**). Many beginners try to test a foothold simply by placing a foot on it; when the foot slips, they give up on the hold. They may reject a dozen footholds in as many seconds in what looks like an attack of some nervous disease. But the fact is that on tiny or sloping holds your foot probably will slide until you commit your weight to the hold. *Friction between your foot and the slope is a force which must be applied.* The only way to test a foothold is to stand on it. It takes experience to learn what you can stand on. While you are learning, expect to slide off holds quite a bit.

There are several ways to use your feet. To some extent the choice of technique will depend on your shoes. Different shoes require somewhat different footwork, depending on their stiffness, the fit, and even the degree of wear on the edges of the soles. To some extent technique is also dictated by the configuration of the rock and the moves to be made. In addition, most climbers develop their own individual styles. In Chapter 2 we saw the distinction between edging and smearing. Whether you edge or smear in a particular situation will depend on all of the considerations above.

The foot acts as a lever, and the length of the lever determines the force or strain on it. If you stand on your heel, the lever effect and the strain are minimized. Climbers don't often climb on their heels; however, a heelhold can be an excellent rest position. If you place the tip of your toe on a tiny hold, *toeing in* to the rock, the strain is at a maximum. Despite the strain, toeing in to the rock is sometimes the best position **(Figure 7)**. More commonly, especially in EB's, you will turn the toe of your shoe to the side, about 45 degrees from straight in, so that more of your big toe is in contact with the rock. Or you may turn the inside edge or even the outside edge of your shoe into the rock so that you are supported by the ball of your foot—the least strenuous of the three positions described. Because the variables are so numerous, it is difficult to formulate principles except for this: *Look at your footholds and position your feet deliberately and precisely.* It is surprising how often beginners will allow their feet to scrape over several inches of rock before settling into position almost by accident. You will need much experimenting to learn the best foot positions for different situations.

Often it is necessary to put both feet in about the same place. Beginners commonly fail to anticipate this situation and will cover two perfectly good footholds with one foot. Plan ahead and leave room for the other foot. Sometimes it is necessary to move one foot carefully and put the other in its place. This can be done with a quick hop or by twisting one foot out of the way just as the other slips into its place.

Apart from careless foot placement an error common to many beginners is standing on the rock with heels lifted up above the toes so that foot and calf muscles are strained **(Figure 3)**. Expert climbers sometimes do this in order to take advantage of the tiniest holds, but it is usually a mistake for beginners. It is a cause of insecurity and "shaky leg." Relax and let your heels down.

Balance Climbing

Balance climbing is the foundation of climbing technique because it makes the least demands on arms and hands. It is the technique necessarily employed for doing climbs "no hands," and no-hands and one-hand climbing are excellent training. Balance climbing should be learned on a beginner's slope. **Figure 3** shows a novice climber making all the mistakes on a low-angle slope. Note carefully the following errors:

1. The novice is leaning into the slope so that his body is pushing his feet outward away from the slope.

2. His body is suspended between two footholds so that neither foot is free to move unless he supports himself with his hands. This position, called *stemming,* is a valuable climbing technique, but it is inappropriate on this slope.

3. His legs are bent and his heels are raised above his toes; thus leg muscles are tensed and tire quickly. His legs may shake, adding to his insecurity.

Figure 3. A novice making all the mistakes on a low-angle slope.

Figure 4a. The rest stance.

4. Sensing that a slide is imminent, he is reaching high for a handhold, which only makes matters worse. To make the reach, he must lean closer to the slope and push outward more on his feet. When the slide comes, the high handhold is immediately out of reach. If he is lucky enough not to slide off the slope, he is unlikely to move upward by pushing with his legs, as his feet are too insecure, so he will try to haul on his arms.

In balance climbing a single move may be thought of as a three-part cycle: (1) a rest position or stance; (2) a shifting of weight from one foot to the other; (3) a lifting movement into a new rest position. **Figures 4a, b,** and **c** show a climber correctly executing these three stages.

In **Figure 4a** the climber is in the initial rest stance. Note:

1. The climber's body is poised over her supporting foot, pushing that foot straight down into the slope. If she must lean into the slope to reach handholds, she bends at the waist and compensates by shifting her hips outward.

2. She has committed all of her weight to the supporting foot, leaving the other foot free to maneuver.

3. Her supporting leg is straight and her heel down so that the leg muscles are relaxed. This leg

Figure 4b. The weight shift.

is resting. The other leg is resting, too, until it begins to lift her body.

4. Her handholds are low and used mainly for balance. If a foot slips, she can recover by leaning over her hands.

In **Figure 4b** the climber has shifted her weight from the straight leg to the leading leg by bending the ankle and knee of the leading leg. There are three ways in which the shifting can be related to the lifting:

1. The climber may shift first, then lift entirely with the leading leg. This makes the maximum demand on leg strength.

2. Alternatively, the climber can make a little spring with the back leg. This is the more natural move. It requires less leg strength but surer control. As I have pointed out, climbing is becoming more dynamic.

3. Beginners will usually haul on their arms before their weight is shifted completely to the leading leg. This climbing out of balance is often necessary, but ideally it is to be avoided. You should not expend hand and arm strength on this slope. Here the hands are for balance.

It is important to complete the lifting movement, that is, to stand all the way up on the lifting leg so that it is straight, as shown in **Figure 4c.**

Figure 4c. The completion of the lift to the next rest stance. Note that the climber's hands have not moved throughout this sequence.

At the same time, the back leg moves forward to the next foothold. Often beginners will lift part way, then hesitate in a sort of crouch and look for a higher handhold. Climbing that way is a desperate business!

Balance climbing is like climbing stairs. It is worth taking a minute to practice on stairs, paying attention to the sequence of movements. Start in the rest position. Then make a neat shift and lift to a new rest stance on the next step. You may recognize this procedure as the *rest step* that is widely employed in hiking uphill and mountaineering because it is an efficient way to ascend a long slope. When you move from the stairs to the rock, the main difference will be not in technique but in the character of the footholds. On a low-angle slope you can stand on almost anything, and you should get used to it.

Balance climbing is the basis of technique on steep slopes. And the position of hips and shoulders is *perhaps the most important single element of technique*. Note carefully the following: On low-angle slopes, like that in **Figure 4,** the climber's hips are ordinarily well away from the slope so that they will be in balance over her feet. Her

Figure 5. In balance under an overhang.

Figure 6. Out of balance on the same holds used in Figure 5.

shoulders may be moved forward so that she can reach handholds. On steep slopes, like that in **Figure 5,** the climber's hips may be pressed forward close to the rock. At the same time, she arches her back and moves her shoulders back away from the rock. Thus, hips forward, shoulders back, and back arched, she is still in balance over her feet. This body position minimizes reliance on hands and arms. It does require a reliable foothold.

Often beginners will fail to complete a move by getting hips and shoulders into balance over feet. Instead, they will stand on bent legs and, what is worse, hang from bent arms. **Figures 5** and **6** show a climber in balance and out of balance, respectively, on the same slope. Note that the climber's hands and feet are employing the same holds in both cases. In Figure 6 she needs only to position and flex her torso to attain the comfortable stance of Figure 5. Note also that her shoulders are lower in Figure 6, and so the next handhold is farther away. Countless beginners

have fallen from exactly this place on Indian Rock trying to go for a handhold, which is still too far away, from a body position that demands too much arm strength. Much of the difficulty of climbing is a problem not of reach and strength but of correct positioning and flexing of the torso.

Where footholds are minimal, it is necessary to move hips away from the rock in order to press feet toward it. This weight shift can be very subtle, as seen in **Figure 7.** The climber is still in balance over tiny edges and making minimal demands on difficult finger holds.

When you are first learning to climb, you should devote most of your time to perfecting your balance climbing technique. Climb up and down and sideways. Practice with only one hand for balance, then with one finger, then no hands. Some beginners are immediately attracted by the challenge of steep slopes and overhangs, but it is a mistake to try to develop basic technique there.

Figure 7. In balance on a steep slope.

No-Hands Climbing

When you have mastered balance climbing, you will no longer need to cling or pull with your hands on a beginner's slope. You can make the transition to no-hands climbing by placing your hands flat against the slope below shoulder level. Use them only to steady your balance. With a little practice you will need only one hand for balance, then none at all.

Putting Your Feet Where Your Hands Are, Mantles, and Exit Moves

Where holds are far apart, it is necessary to move your feet up a smooth slope to the same level as your hands, perhaps even placing a foot on the same small hold as a hand and balancing up. You may be able to keep your feet on the slope by hanging back against your hands so that your body is out away from the rock and thus pressing your feet in toward it. This is climbing out of balance. You get back into balance by putting a foot on a high hold and rolling your body up over it **(Figures 8a, b,** and **c).** This takes less strength if it is done dynamically, that is, quickly with a bit of spring. You are now in a crouch over one leg, and can stand up. The maneuver just described is a kind of *lieback,* though it is not usually called that. (See p. 43 for a discussion of liebacking.) On steep slopes it requires a handhold that you can pull outward on; a flat ledge will not do.

Figure 8. Using a lieback to gain a ledge.

8a.

8b.

8c.

Suppose you have only a flat ledge. There are no intermediate footholds, and you cannot walk your feet up the slope because that will pull your hands off the ledge. A strenuous maneuver called a *mantleshelf*, or just a *mantle*, is required. You must pull your body up with your arms until your head is above your hands **(Figure 9a)**, then turn a hand (or both hands) until your palm is on the ledge and you can begin to push your body still higher with your arm. When you are heaved up as high as possible above your hands **(Figure 9b)**, lift a foot to the ledge and stand up **(Figure 9d)**. If the mantle ledge is narrow and there are no handholds on the slope above, then what started out as a strenuous maneuver may become a delicate balance act.

A pure mantle is a strenuous maneuver indeed. Many women lack the strength in their wrists and shoulders for this maneuver. Fortunately, the need for a pure mantle is rare; usually there are other ways of solving the same problem. Usually it is possible to walk your feet at least part way up the slope **(Figure 9a)**. Then any little thing in the way of a foothold, often something out to the side, will take some of your weight and ease the strenuous transition from pulling with your arms to pushing. There are various body twisting stratagems for making this transition easier.

Much of the art of mantling consists in choosing exactly the right places for your hands and for the foot that you will balance up on. Often a beginner will put a hand on the only feasible place for the foot but discovers this only after he has heaved up over his hands. If you will be able to get a hand up to a good hold above the mantle ledge, then most anything will do for the foot. However, if you must do a delicate balance act, you had better leave the best place free for your foot.

9b.

9a.

Figure 9. Mantling to gain a ledge.

9c.

9d.

Figure 10. Mantling on tiny holds.

Mantling is a powerful technique. It permits climbing where holds are far apart, perhaps seven feet or more. It is often necessary for mounting the lip of an overhang. It is possible to mantle on almost any kind of hold provided the slope above is not too steep: extremely narrow ledges, steeply sloping ledges, or even two or three tiny but closely spaced holds. **Figure 10** illustrates a mantle on extremely tiny holds. It is easier to support your body entirely by pushing down against one palm (supporting arm straight, elbow locked), as shown in **Figure 9c,** than by hanging from one arm. However, mantling is strenuous, delicate, and committing all at once. A mantle is not always easily reversed if the climber gets part way up and then discovers he cannot do it.

You can practice mantling on man-made walls and on the narrow ledges along the sides of buildings. The most strenuous kind of mantling—mounting the lip of an overhang—can be learned on the edge of a heavy table or the overhang of a roof.

More common than mantles and much easier, though still troublesome for beginners, are what I call *exit moves*. These occur where a steep slope suddenly lies back to near horizontal, as in climbing onto a large ledge or the top of a cliff. There are no handholds to reach *up* for. The beginner will reach *forward* for a handhold, which often isn't there. If it is there, using it may be awkward. The beginner will lose sight and contact with his footholds, then belly flop onto the ledge **(Figure 11).** In the exit situation don't reach forward; keep your hands near the brink **(Figure 12a).** Look for footholds and walk your feet up or mantle if necessary. As in mantling, get your shoulders over your palms **(Figure 12b)** and push your body up until your arms are straight. Then place a foot on the brink and stand up **(Figure 12c).**

Figure 12. Making an exit move correctly.

Figure 11. A novice making mistakes on an exit move.

12a.

12b.

12c.

Stemming

So far I have talked as if you always strive to keep your body poised over one foot. That is the way to move with the least reliance on arms and hands. You may pause or rest supported by both feet; you may lift your body with both legs. But you cannot advance a foot to the next hold until you either get into balance over the other foot or else lean against an arm. The only other possibility is a quick, precise kick!

Stemming, or *bridging* (the latter term is used mostly by British climbers), is a variation on balance climbing where your feet are spread wide apart horizontally. Both feet may be on the same

level, or one foot may be under you and the other far and high to the side. In the former case your weight will be distributed between your feet; in the latter it will be largely on the lower foot. The classic application of stemming is in climbing very wide cracks or *chimneys* **(Figure 13).** You ascend with one hand and foot pressing against each wall of the chimney, your body poised in space between the two walls. The walls are said to be *opposed* toward each other, your feet employed *in opposition* to each other. We will consider a variety of opposition techniques (also called *cross-pressure* or *counterpressure*) in later sections.

Figure 13. Stemming a wide chimney.

The classic application of stemming suggests another less obvious application of the technique. Ordinary balance climbing requires at least footholds you can press down on. Stemming makes it possible to climb steep faces where there are surfaces against which you must press sideways **(Figures 14a–e).** There must be two holds—either hand- or footholds—far enough apart horizontally that you can suspend your body between them. Of course, stemming can also be done on ledges or slopes you can press down on. Whether you employ stemming or ordinary balance technique will depend simply on which is easier for a given move. You may shift quickly from one to the other.

14b.

14a.

Figure 14. Stemming on a steep face.

14c.

14d.

14e.

Figure 15. Stemming a dihedral using push–pull combinations.

15a.

A configuration of rock where two faces or walls come together at more or less a right angle, like the corner of a room, is called an *inside corner*, a *dihedral*, or an *open book* (after the Open Book route at Tahquitz Rock in Southern California). You may ascend the crack where the two walls come together or climb on one side or the other. However, stemming between the two walls is often the most elegant and least strenuous method for climbing a dihedral **(Figures 15a, b, c)**.

Stemming is also commonly employed in crack climbing. You may have one foot jammed in the crack and the other on the face to one side. However, beginners will often try to stem where they should have both feet in the crack, particularly with offwidth cracks (see Offwidth Cracks).

On steep slopes and dihedrals the stemming position provides lateral stability without the need to rely on your hands. Thus you can often get both hands off the rock to rest or place protection. The stemming position is indispensable for the long, fatiguing task of drilling a bolt hole on a steep face.

Stemming requires a sophisticated use of the hands in order to free a foot for upward movement. The simplest case is the wide chimney, where you support your body by pushing outward against both walls with your hands (opposition) while you lift a foot. Often, however, you will employ *push-pull combinations* with your hands. As you lift the left foot, your left hand will push against the rock low and to the left side; the right hand may be clinging or pulling on either side of your body. In effect, the pushing hand is being used in opposition to the other (right) foot. Then the left foot may move to the same hold and

15b.

15c.

take the place of the pushing hand. Having moved your left foot up, you will then pull with the left hand, push with the right, lift the right foot, and so on. Push-pull combinations are so useful that you should make a deliberate study of the technique; it is illustrated in **Figures 15b** and **14a–c.**

Sometimes it is easiest to free a foot, say the left one, by bringing the right foot across to the same side and placing it near the left foot. You will be pushing hard against your right hand. Then the left foot moves up, and the right foot goes back to the right into the stemming position again.

Using Your Hands

Beginners invariably reach up for a horizontal edge of rock they can pull down on with their fingers. Often it's not necessary to reach high; such *cling holds* are also useful when they are situated quite low relative to your body. You should look, too, for diagonal or vertical edges you can pull sideways on, either toward your body or away from it. These *sidecling holds* are often less tiring to fingers and forearms than horizontal ledges because there is less tendency to hang from them.

You may also use an inverted edge or *undercling hold*, which you pull up on **(Figure 16a).** An undercling may be difficult to use when you first reach for it but improve as you move past it. In general, some handholds become less secure as you move past them, while others improve. Often a beginner will reject a perfectly good hold in the latter category because it seems awkward or insecure when he first reaches for it. Spend

Figure 16. Using an undercling hold and a foot jam on an overhang.

some time experimenting with holds. The test of a hold is not that you can hang onto it but that you can move from it to the next holds.

Beginners suppose that clinging demands strong arms and fingers. Strength is important, and climbers develop it. However, a beginner's hands usually slip off the rock not because he lacks strength but because he has not learned how to grip effectively. Many beginners hold on with only three fingers; neither thumb nor pinkie finger is on the rock. Your pinkie is not strong, but it does help. More important, *your thumb is your strongest finger, and you should always use it* **(Figure 17a).**

Often there is an obvious point of support for your thumb. It is frequently possible to squeeze the rock between your thumb and fingers; this powerful technique is called the *pinch grip* **(Figure 18).** If there is no separate thumb hold or pinch grip, your grip will be strengthened if you push the end of your thumb against the end of your index finger or (on tiny holds) clamp it down on top of the index finger. In either case the two fingers will make a ring **(Figure 19).**

16a.

16b.

Figure 17a. Cling holds. Note the tight configuration of fingers and the use of thumbs and pinkies for maximum strength.

Figure 17b. Hand hooks. Thumbs, palms, and fists can be pressed or hooked on the rock in various ways to rest fingers.

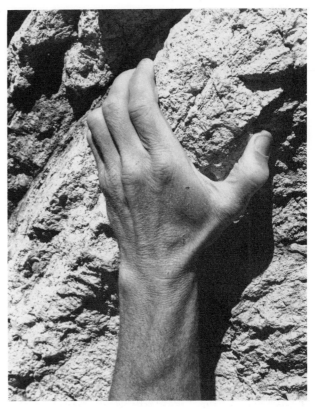

Figure 18. A pinch grip.

Figure 19. A ring grip.

Figure 20. A grip with the base of the palm.

On very poor handholds each finger may seek out its own point of support, resulting in an open configuration of the hand. More useful in most situations is a closed configuration: you should press your fingers tightly together or even, on tiny holds, press one finger down on another *(stacked fingers)* to make a strong grip. Your fingers may lie flush with the rock or they may be bent so that, with the thumb pressed against the index finger, your hand is cupped. The ends of the fingers and the base of your palm are pressed against the rock **(Figure 20).** Often grip is improved and your body more stable if your forearm also lies against the rock (see **Figure 7).**

On larger holds you can cling with the side or edge of your hand away from your thumb or with the base of it. If you use the base of your hand, your wrist will be bent so that your hand and arm make a sort of hook **(Figure 17b).** In either case you may be able to grip the rock without using your fingers, thus allowing them to rest. I sometimes make a tight fist, grip the rock with the outside of the bent index finger, and pull toward my body with it or lean against it, thereby resting my fingers.

You can push with your hands as well as cling with them. We have already met *push holds*

in mantling, stemming, and push-pull combinations (see Stemming). Ordinarily your hand will be low, and you will push downward, inward, or sideways. However, when you are below an overhang, you may hold yourself on the rock by pushing upward or even outward on it.

Hands are often used in opposition: pulling toward one another, pulling away from one another, or pushing away from each other.

There are countless ways to wedge your fingers or hands in cracks; we will consider these in the succeeding sections on crack-climbing technique.

Sometimes both hands must use the same hold at the same time. Remember to leave room for them both.

Counterbalance

Handholds and footholds serve two purposes. First, and obviously, they are things to pull and push on. Second, and less obviously, they

Figure 21. Using counterbalance on a steep face.

21a.

serve to *distribute the climber's weight* in some tenable fashion, preferably in balance over one or both feet. Sometimes you should choose a hold not because it is easy to grip or press against, but because it is in the right place to give the needed weight distribution or balance. For example, in stepping up to the right, you will naturally reach in the same direction for a handhold. The reaching is part of getting into balance over the foot.

You may make the reach in the desired direction *even if there isn't any hold to reach for.* Your arm or leg will simply lie against the rock or be suspended in space in order to give the needed balance. I will call this technique *counterbalance.* The example above seems obvious, but it is nonetheless contrary to the instinctive need of the beginner to cling to a good hold—even when it is in the wrong place. It is also contrary to the oft-repeated maxim that the climber should keep three points of contact with the rock. Much hard climbing is hard exactly because it requires the climber to rely on only one or two points of contact. Even on easier terrain the climber moving fluidly and efficiently will frequently have only two points of contact.

Counterbalance is simply a dynamic view of balance climbing. The principle is this: Movement of one part of your body requires a compensating or counter movement of other parts in order to maintain balance. Hips and shoulders are employed as well as arms and legs; for example, you may balance a long reach to the right by moving hips or a leg to the left. **Figures 21a–c** illustrate a classic application of counterbalance. The climber must step up with the left foot onto a hold that slopes down to the right. The only handhold within reach is low and to the right. The next higher handhold is still farther right. She manages this move by shifting her torso hard left and keeping a foot out to the right (no foothold, but pressing in against the rock) to maintain balance over the supporting foot. Without the shift left she would have to employ enormous arm and shoulder strength. Without the foot to the right she would rotate off the rock. As it is, the move is a balance act requiring little strength.

21b.

21c.

On steep rock you will often feel a tendency to swing or rotate off the rock—*barn door* off is the expression climbers use. You can resist this tendency by applying strength. But it may be better to move with it. If your body wants to swing to the right out of control, then shift some part of it to the right deliberately. **Figure 22** illustrates a long reach to the left from a lieback on a radical overhang. The climber has swung her body round to the left to reach the left handhold. She resists the tendency to swing back right by keeping a leg out to the right and pressed against the rock (no foothold).

Relating Your Body to the Available Holds

There are two ways to climb, and all the difference in the world between them. Many climbers simply hunt for the next hold and climb past it, hoping that hold will be located where they need it and will be more or less adequate. They reject perfectly good holds which seem to be in the wrong place or to slope the wrong way.

More expert climbers have learned that climbing is not a matter of hunting and hauling.

Rather, it is the imaginative use of what is available. They survey the rock, noting every hold, then move their bodies into the best relationship with the available holds.

Relating to holds involves leaning this way and that, crouching, bending, twisting, arching the back. It uses the shoulders and hips as well as the arms and legs. It resembles popular dance. Shoulders and hips move in and out, side to side, up and down, enabling the climber to pull on or push against each hold from the most secure direction. Often the climber is deliberately out of balance; however, out-of-balance movements should be regarded as transitions between stances in balance.

I like to tell the story of the boulderer whose foot kept slipping off a particular hold. Along came the local expert. "Your thumb is in the wrong place," he said. The boulderer shifted his thumb to the appointed position, and his foot stayed on the rock. The story sounds farfetched. But in fact a pinch grip allowed the climber to lean against his hand just enough more to keep his foot on a tenuous hold.

Figure 22. A lieback and counterbalance on a radical overhang.

Figure 23. Liebacking a crack.

Figure 24. Liebacking a crack with one foot on the face to the side.

Climbing Out of Balance

Climbing out of balance means leaning outward or sideways against your arm so that it supports a significant portion of your weight. We have already encountered it in walking your feet up a smooth slope and in stemming. It is widely employed in crack climbing and is perforce the way up overhangs.

You can (and often should) lean outward or sideways *without throwing your weight against your arms,* or by weighting them only slightly. This is done by bending at the waist or arching your back. It is the way to take advantage of awkwardly located or sloping holds as described in the preceding section. Many climbers hang against handholds when they don't need to. They tire quickly on pitches the more expert climber finds not at all strenuous. They think he is stronger because he doesn't tire, but actually he avoids using his arm and hand strength.

The classic application of climbing out of balance is the *lieback.* This technique is used for

climbing a crack in a corner or a crack with one edge offset from the other. In **Figure 23** the climber grasps one edge of the crack with both hands, leans back against her arms, and walks her feet up the opposite side of the crack. Thus she pulls sideways with her hands and pushes in the opposite direction with her feet. In this fashion hands and feet alternate in making small advances upward. On steep cracks the climber's arms are straight, so that muscles are relaxed, and her feet are lifted to a level a little below her butt.

A steep lieback is both strenuous and committing. Once you have started, it is not easy to rest, place protection, or shift to jamming the crack. Before undertaking a lieback you should consider the alternatives: balance climbing, stemming, jamming, or back-and-knee chimney technique (for the last two, see Crack Climbing). It may be best to take advantage of holds on the face to the side **(Figure 24).** Sometimes you will be leaning back against your hands but stemming

25a.

25b.

Figure 25. Moving from a lieback into stemming on an overhang.

with your legs. These combination techniques require more careful footwork, but they may save much strain on your hands and arms.

The lieback is also useful on faces and overhangs. Then usually just one side of the climber's body is involved in the lieback, while a hand reaches for a hold above or to the other side. Such a lieback may enable a long reach to the side (**Figures 25a** and **b.** See also **Figure 22**).

Once you are committed to a lieback, move forward boldly and steadily.

Traverses

The techniques for moving sideways *(traversing)* are the same as those for moving upward, but with a different emphasis. Sideclinging holds, opposed holds (hands pulling either toward or away from one another), liebacks, stemming, and counterbalance are commonplace on traverses. *Heel hooks* (**Figure 26**) and *toe hooks*, rarely employed to move upward, are useful when you must reach or lie out far to the side. Often you will lieback or use counterbalance to make a long reach to the side. Such a move usually leads into the stemming position (see **Figures 25a** and **b**).

Since you usually face toward the rock, on a traverse one side of your body will be leading and the other side trailing. The hand and foot on the leading side ordinarily stay in the lead as you step sideways. However, both hands or both feet may have to occupy a hold at the same time. You must plan ahead for this either by leaving a place on the hold for the trailing hand or foot or by managing an adroit exchange. I sometimes pick up the fingers of one hand one at a time just as the fingers of the other hand replace them one at a time.

Figure 26. Using a heel hook on an overhang.

27a.

Figure 27. Exchanging feet on a traverse.

Crossing a hand or foot either in front of or behind its mate can be useful on traverses. A well-known climbing manual shows a cartoon climber crossing one foot behind the other and labels this procedure incorrect. This is one of my favorite maneuvers.

There are no rules in climbing except this: Do whatever works for you and conserves strength. Climbers come in different sizes and shapes. They have varying strengths and skills. They have developed different styles. It is amazing to see the different methods climbers will use on the same stretch of rock. These differences are especially evident on traverses. At a favorite Indian Rock traverse the crux move is a very long step off of an awkwardly sloping foothold. The first problem is to change feet on this hold or somehow pass it. One local climber makes a neat hop **(Figures 27a, b, c).** Another turns sideways to the rock and simply steps through to the next foothold with the trailing foot. I leave room on the original foothold and cross behind the leading foot with the trailing foot as the climber in **Figure 28** is doing.

27b.

27c.

Figure 28. Crossing one foot behind the other on the same foothold used in Figure 27b.

Overhangs

In recent years *overhangs* and *ceilings* have become the *sine qua non* of the hardest routes and boulder problems. Actually, many of these overhangs are not so much difficult as intimidating. The climber is severely out of balance for an extended time, and that takes getting used to.

Four principles especially apply to climbing overhangs:

1. *Keep your feet on the rock.* Occasionally counterbalance will require swinging a leg into space. Rarely, it is easiest to let both feet at once swing through space to new holds. However, you will not hang from your arms alone for long. Your feet support much of your weight even on radical overhangs. Foot jams (or foot locks), heel hooks, and toe hooks are especially effective this way (see **Figures 16b** and **26**).

One of the surest ways to lose your foothold is to reach too far for a handhold or pull too vig-orously on it. On radical overhangs moves often must be made slowly to prevent your body from swinging out of control.

2. *Plan moves carefully.* The sequence of hand- and footholds can be crucial on overhangs since it is usually difficult to change hands or feet on a hold.

3. Just as a straight leg causes the least muscle fatigue in ordinary balance climbing, so straight arms allow muscles to rest and conserve strength on overhangs. *Keep your arms straight as much as possible* by hanging down or back against your handholds **(Figures 29** and **26).** This is necessary also in order to see crucial footholds **(Figure 12a),** and in order to press feet against holds on an overhang. Compare carefully the right foot positions in **Figures 29** and **30.** In Figure 30 the right foot is about to swing back off of the hold.

4. Even on radical overhangs leg strength is more effective than arm strength. *Lift your body* (i.e., push) *with your feet as much as possible.* For

Figure 29. Hanging back against handholds on an overhang.

Figure 30. Pulling in with the arms on the same overhang shown in Figure 29.

this your feet must be high and close in to your body. Your legs will be bent **(Figure 32).** Note carefully how the climber in **Figures 25a** and **b** has raised her body without bending her arms.

Figure 30 illustrates the most common error in dealing with overhangs. Beginners will pull in to the rock with their arms, lose sight of the rock below their noses, then perforce haul themselves upward with their arms.

Figure 31 illustrates the technique for resting an arm on an overhang. Note carefully how the climber has moved her butt in close to her heels in order to press her feet against tiny footholds and gain maximum support from them, thus relieving some of the strain on hand and shoulder. She has done the same thing with the left foot in Figure 29. This is an important, though often overlooked, technique.

Figure 32. Keeping feet high on an overhang

Figure 31. Resting one arm on an overhang.

Crack Climbing

Cracks come in every conceivable width, shape, and relation to the rock they penetrate. Some are uniform for fifty or a hundred feet, requiring repetition of the same moves. Others change shape or direction dramatically, requiring the climber to modify the technique with every move. Sometimes cracks require quite bizarre moves. The possibilities are endlessly varied; the crack climber must be imaginative and experimental. In the following sections I will treat only the simplest and most common cases. Except where specifically noted, I will be dealing with cracks that run straight up the rock and with techniques mainly as they are related to crack width.

Except for the lieback you climb a crack by lodging or jamming your body or some part of it inside the crack. The problem is very similar to placing chocks (see Chockcraft, Chapter 4). The easiest solution is to wedge fingers, hand, fist, arm, shoulder, toes, foot, or leg above a constriction in the crack. You can also pull or push up against a constriction. If there isn't a constriction you must find some way of jamming the body part by *torquing* or *camming* it. A hand or foot may be slipped sideways into a narrow crack, then twisted around (torqued) to tighten in place. Hand, arm, foot, or leg may be flexed to exert pressure against both sides of a crack. One body part may be used to wedge another (usually the fingers) tightly against the rock.

The general principles of face climbing apply as well to cracks: Climb mainly with your feet. Try to keep in balance. Keep your hands low as much as possible. Lean this way and that, move shoulders and hips in and out, and so on to make the best use of holds. Again, there are no hard rules except to do whatever works for you and conserves strength.

The difficulty of a crack and your choice of technique depend in part on the size and shape of your body. A woman with small hands may slip her fingers into a tiny crack where a man with large hands can get no hold at all. The man may get solid fist jams in a wider crack where the woman must resort to offwidth technique. Because cracks are continuous features, height is not generally an advantage in crack climbing. On the other hand, small size and light weight probably are.

Crack climbing, even more than face climbing, is a learned art. While you are learning, expect to struggle, thrash, hurt, and become frustrated. Cracks can be painful, abrasive, or injurious. Many climbers use adhesive tape to protect the backs of their hands and wrists from abrasions. An ill-managed fall can result in a sprained wrist or dislocated shoulder when feet come away from a crack and an arm remains lodged in it. Be assured that with patience, discipline, and practice it will all become easier—even elegant.

There are two "first principles" of crack climbing. The first is the patience and discipline. A *jam* or *lock* is not as obvious or easy as other kinds of holds. You must take the time and trouble to "set" the jam correctly and securely before you go for the next hold. Don't rush the climbing unless you know exactly what you are doing.

The second principle is difficult to master. It requires thoughtful experimentation and practice. Some finger and hand jams become more secure as you move up on them, whereas others tend to give way. *You should seek a hold that tends to improve;* otherwise you will waste a lot of strength trying to maintain a bad hold. Beginners can exhaust themselves climbing a crack that requires no strength at all, only the right technique.

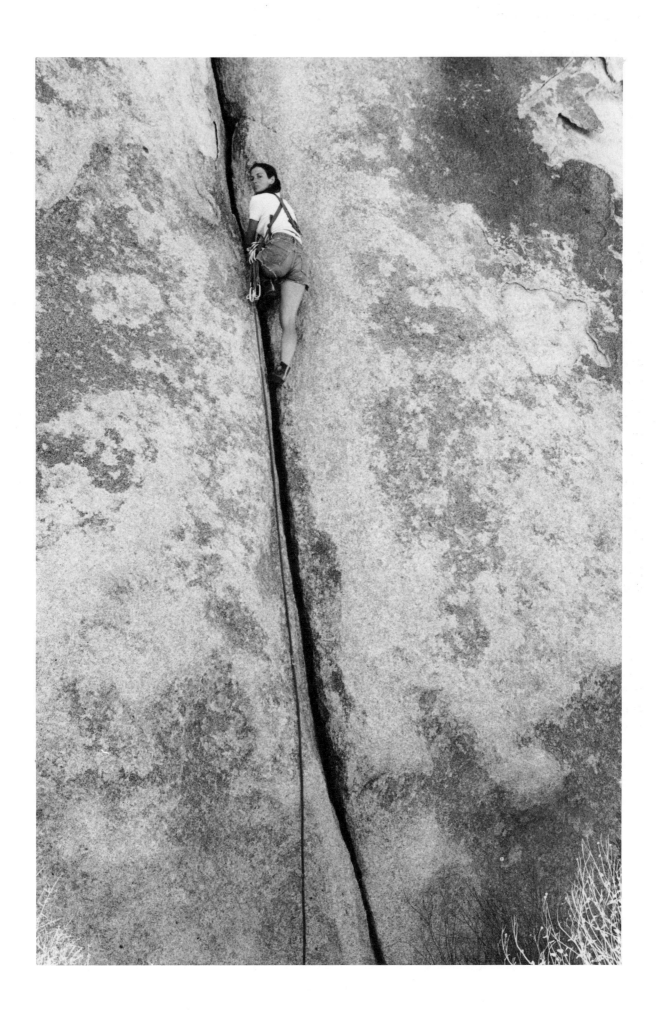

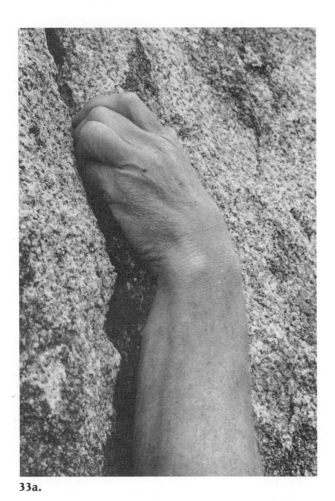

33a.

33b.

Figure 33. A pinkie jam in a crack, and the hand configuration for it.

Finger Cracks
(to about 1½ inches)

Climbing *finger cracks* is similar to face climbing. The crack itself offers minimal footholds, so look for them on the face to either side. If the crack is in a corner or the two edges are offset, you may be able to lieback. However, liebacking a steep, thin crack is strenuous. If the crack is not too steep, a useful variation on the lieback consists of keeping one foot in the crack and the other on the face to the side (see **Figure 24**). You may pull leftward against the left edge of the crack with both hands while you push rightward against the right edge with your right foot (toes pointing up). Your body will be to the left of the crack and your left foot on the face underneath it. This technique is often less tiring than trying to toe in to a thin crack with poor toe holds and finger jams. It can be used for climbing pin scars.

Finger jams or *locks* are the key to thin cracks. In the thinnest crack you will be able to lodge only your pinkie (with the thumb of the hand up). This *pinkie jam* **(Figures 33a, b)** is a surprisingly strong hold if you stack the rest of your fingers firmly on top of the pinkie. Each should be turned so that the pad of the finger is down and the nail up. For wider cracks slip your fingers farther in and obtain a torquing or tightening action by lifting your elbow up and to the side of the crack. The elbow rises automatically as you move upward; thus the pinkie jam improves as you move past it. Often you can move quite high on it and make a long reach with the other hand. It also improves if you lean to the same side as the hand you are using, that is, lean left against a left-hand pinkie jam. If you lean to the right in this situation, you must make a conscious effort to keep your elbow up and hand torqued, or you will simply be gripping one edge of the crack. This works if you can keep a grip on the edge but is strenuous.

If the crack is wide enough to admit your index finger, a *ring jam* may be used **(Figures 34a, b).** In this case your hand is turned so that the thumb is down, and your other fingers are stacked on top of the index finger. Then press the

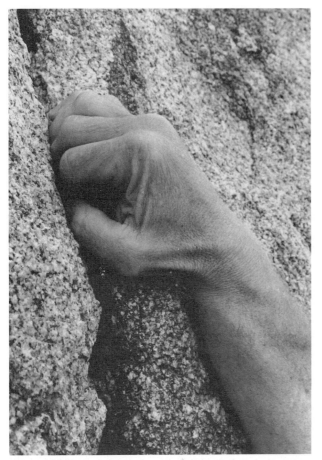

34a.

34b.

Figure 34. A ring jam in a crack, and the hand configuration for it.

tip of your thumb toward your index finger, making a ring with these two fingers. Your thumb may or may not fit into the crack. The ring jam is torqued by keeping your wrist turned downward and pressed against the rock. It is a remarkably versatile hold. It works in a wide range of crack widths, and, within limits, you can make long reaches both for it and from it and lean either way on it.

An important variation for cracks in the 1- to 1½-inch range, depending on the width of your fingers, is the *thumb cam* **(Figure 35).** Place your thumb in the crack pointing the tip upward and pressing the pad against one side. Then wedge your index finger tightly between the thumb and the other side of the crack. Stack the other fingers on top to the extent possible. The thumb cam is a difficult hold but very useful when a crack of the appropriate width has particularly smooth, parallel sides.

See also Cracks that Lean and Cracks in Corners and Flares.

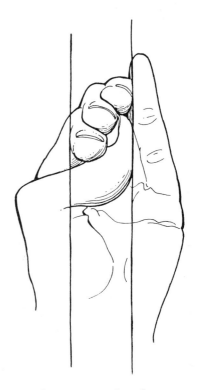

Figure 35. A thumb cam.

Figure 36. Toe jams.

Hand and Fist Cracks
(about 1½ to 4 inches)

It is important to get a foot in a crack as soon as possible. When a crack is about 1½ inches wide, you will be able to lodge the tip of your toe in it; on thinner cracks you can gain a limited purchase by taking advantage of offsets, flares, and other irregularities. Make a *toe jam* by turning your foot sideways (big toe up and knee out to the side) and slipping the toe into the crack. Then torque the toe jam by pulling your knee back up toward the crack and straightening your body up **(Figure 36).** In wider cracks the toe jam becomes a *foot jam*.

A toe or foot jam is less tiring if you can stand tall and get into balance, with hips forward and shoulders back on a steep slope. The other foot may be on a hold or simply pressed against the face to the side. Often you will need only one hand in the crack and it will be low, perhaps as low as your waist, and turned so that the thumb is up as described below. It will be especially se-

Figure 37. Jamming a hand crack.

37a.

cure if it is set just *below* a constriction and is pulling upward against it. This is the preferred stance for resting and placing protection. **Figures 37a–e** show two moves up a classic jamcrack. However, on steeper and harder cracks you may have to keep your feet close in to your body and hang down against your hand jams (see **Figure 32**).

Climbers commonly "walk" their feet up a crack by placing each foot in turn above the other. Alternatively, you may make smaller, less awkward moves, leaning less on your hands, by "shuffling" your feet—that is, keeping one always ahead of the other. Of course, you can shift from walking to shuffling as the case requires or as a matter of personal style.

37c.

37b.

37e.

37d.

When your hands go into the crack, the thumb may be turned either up or down. Thumb up is the classic *hand jam* **(Figure 38).** For convenience I will continue to call the thumb-down configuration a ring jam, although in this version more of the hand is inside the crack and thumb and index finger may not make a ring. The characteristics and uses of these two jams are quite different. However, there are some common points.

In both hand and ring jams the jam will be stronger if you can lodge the base of your hand in the crack. Your wrist may be bent so that hand and arm make a sort of hook and your fingers are pointing into the crack or even downward slightly. For the purpose of visibility the fingers in **Figure 38** are pointing up the crack. In reality, with a hand jam the hand will ordinarily be turned into the crack more. With a ring jam the fingers may be pointing up the crack. The latter configuration is especially broad and strong if your thumb is flattened against your palm.

In either case you can flex your hand, making a sort of cup. In wider cracks you can flex your wrist so that fingers are pressed against one side and the back of your wrist or arm against the other. You may be able to lodge a closed fist. You will find *fist jams* painful and may not want to trust them, but a good fist jam is a very secure hold. Tuck your thumb against your palm, slip your hand into the crack, make a tight fist, and turn the fist as needed. It may be lodged in the crack with the thumb up, down, or to either side. Take advantage of even the slightest constrictions in the crack to make a secure jam. You can make a wider fist by keeping your thumb outside and pressed against the side of the index finger. This configuration is not as secure, however.

Now for the differences between the hand and ring jams. You cannot torque a hand jam when you are hanging down against your arm, so hand jams (thumb up) do not work well high above your head unless you can lodge the base of your hand against a constriction. They often do work well quite low, perhaps as low as your

knees; you can make long reaches *from* a hand jam. The converse may be said of ring jams. A hand jam is more secure if you lean to the same side as the hand you are using, as you will tend to do in reaching up with the other hand. Often it is helpful to exaggerate this lean (see **Figure 37b**). Ordinarily you can lean either way on a ring jam.

As a consequence of the differences, the two most common procedures for jamming are:

1. Both hands are kept relatively low or close in to your body, both turned with the thumb up (hand jams), each moving past the other to the next jam **(Figures 37a–e).** If you are having trouble reaching the next jam, simply set the new jam *below* the other hand.

2. One hand may be quite high above your head, the other low and close in. The lead hand is turned thumb down (a ring jam), the trailing hand thumb up. They remain in the same position relative to each other, that is, shuffling **(Figure 39).**

Figure 38. A hand jam.

Figure 39. Jamming a right-leaning crack.

Figure 40. A jamming–stemming combination in a corner.

Cracks that Lean and Cracks in Corners and Flares
(of most widths)

Even a subtle leaning of a crack to the right or left will require modification of technique. In general, if a crack leans one way, the hand on that side will need to stay in the lead and the foot on that side will likely stay on the face to that side; in other words, with a right-leaning crack the right hand will lead and the right foot will be on the face **(Figure 39)**.

Corners and flares offer a variety of possibilities for crack climbing: stemming, liebacking, jamming, chimney technique, and combinations of these techniques. Often the combinations will permit you to free one or both hands. Two of the most useful combination techniques are illustrated in **Figures 40** and **41.**

Figure 41. A jamming–chimneying combination in a corner.

Offwidth Cracks
(about 4 to 10 inches)

At about the 4-inch width a crack becomes too wide for foot jams and fist jams. From 4 to 10 inches, however, it is still too narrow to admit the climber's whole body. Cracks in this range are called *offwidth*. Offwidth cracks have a special reputation among climbers because they require a technique which seems difficult to master; many good climbers have never succeeded. In the absence of correct technique these cracks are arduous at best.

There is an interesting history to the evolution of hard free climbs in the United States. The early, now "classic," hard climbs followed obvious crack-and-chimney systems—for example, the Lost Arrow Chimney and the Steck-Salathé Route on the north face of Sentinel Rock, in Yosemite. The hardest pitches were offwidth cracks and chimneys (wider than 10 inches). These were hard because they were difficult to aid or to protect, they were strenuous, and they required a seemingly mysterious technique. At the same time, with the right technique chimneys and offwidth were reasonably secure without protection. Thinner cracks were easier to protect, and, if truly difficult, they were also easier to aid. For years the ability to do hard chimneys and offwidth was the trademark of the Yosemite expert. Today the favored hard climbs are steep faces, thin cracks, and overhangs. Many climbers consider chimneys and offwidth cracks inelegant and avoid them. Good chimney and offwidth technique may be less prevalent than it used to be.

When a crack becomes too wide for fist and foot jams, you must insert an arm into the crack and begin to turn your foot (already in the crack) sideways. As your arm goes into the crack, you will naturally turn sideways, so that you have an inside arm and foot (in the crack) and an outside arm and foot (outside the crack). Which way you face usually makes a difference, but it is difficult to generalize; crack width, flare, lean, and offset all come into play. A randomly placed hold may be important for resting or for a crux move, and it may dictate how you face. Before you start a chimney or an offwidth crack, look ahead and think carefully about which way you will face. In one case a climber failed to climb a particular chimney on three separate occasions because she was facing the wrong way (the same way) each time.

Figure 42. In an offwidth crack using a heel–toe jam with the outside foot.

Your outside leg is the key to offwidth technique (see **Figure 42**). It does the work of lifting your body. The foot spans the crack between the heel and toe, the heel lifted above the toe if possible and turned somewhat into the crack. Sometimes climbers get a good *heel-toe jam* with this foot and then find that they can't move. It is important that your knee be turned *out* (as it will be if your heel is turned in) so that there is space for it when you move your foot higher. Indeed, if your whole body is turned out a little, not only will you be able to work your outside leg more easily, but also your inside leg and arms will be more secure. *These support you while you move the outside foot* to a higher heel-toe jam. When this jam is carefully set, lift your body with the outside leg, and so on. Small upward movements between heel-toe jams are usually best.

Beginners may get careless with the heel-toe jam. Then when it isn't holding, they will try for a foothold on the face to the side. Even if there is a good hold out there, this is a mistake unless that foot is situated to push you *into* the crack. Otherwise, you will be, in effect, on an overhang,

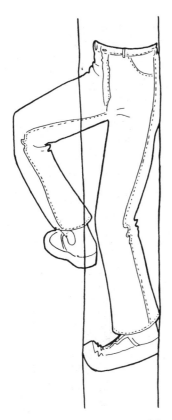

Figure 43. Use of feet and legs in an offwidth crack.

Figure 44. Use of hands and arms in a flaring offwidth crack.

and your inside leg and arms will keep you from falling backward only by pressing very hard against the sides of the crack. Of course, you should take advantage of holds for the outside foot as long as they are directly under your body.

Frequently your inside foot is more or less useless. If there is a foothold or a jam inside the crack, using it *may* only tend to push you out of the crack, though occasionally such a hold is crucial. However, your inside *leg* does help support you by pressing against both sides of the crack at once in a *leg bar*. There are several ways to do this: opposite pressure between foot and knee with knee turned either in or out; between foot and hip; between knee and hip; and so on. In most cases this leg is lifted up and bent at the knee **(Figure 43).**

The use of your arms and hands will vary depending on crack width and flare, but this much can be said: *One hand will be used near shoulder or head level and the other near hip level.* In thinner offwidth cracks the outside hand probably will be the higher one and pulling sideways against the edge of the crack. The inside hand will be low, thumb turned into the crack and palm pressing in the direction you are facing. In wider or flaring offwidth cracks your outside hand will be low, thumb turned away from the crack and palm pushing downward **(Figure 44).** The inside arm may extend more or less straight into the crack, or it may be bent acutely at the elbow. In any case, opposite pressure between your hand and upper arm or shoulder will make an *arm bar* spanning the crack **(Figure 44).**

Remember that your arms and inside leg hold you in place while you move your outside foot a few inches upward. You can waste a lot of energy trying to haul yourself up with your arms. As much as possible, the outside foot should do the work of lifting your body. Done properly, offwidth technique is usually less strenuous than hand jams. Certainly it can be as elegant. I have climbed overhanging offwidth cracks where it is possible to set the foot and legs properly, then lean out from the crack with both hands free. I have yet to see an overhanging hand crack where you can get both hands free!

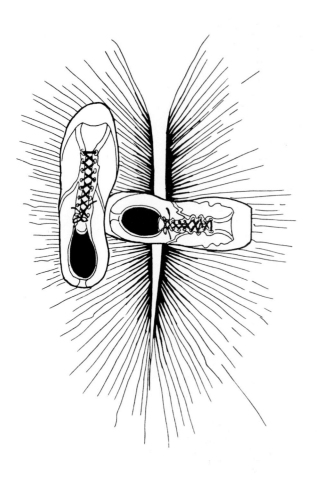

Figure 45. Stacked feet in a squeeze chimney.

Figure 46. Climbing a squeeze chimney.

Chimneys
(cracks wider than 10 inches)

If any climbing problem is inelegant, it is the crack which is a little too wide for a heel-toe jam, at which point it becomes a chimney. Unless a lieback is reasonable (usually it isn't), there is nothing to do but insert your body sideways into the crack. You support yourself by stacking your feet **(Figure 45)** or by spanning the crack with your lower legs. Your knees press painfully against the wall in front of you, your feet against the wall behind **(Figure 46).** Many climbers wear knee pads in *squeeze chimneys.* Arms are used very much as in offwidth cracks, either pushing down in front of you or else spanning the crack between palm and upper arm with an arm bar. Upward progress is slow and strenuous through some manner of squirming because there isn't room to maneuver.

In *flared chimneys,* which are wide toward the outside but narrow inward, beginners will trade maneuverability for security by moving back into the narrowest part of the chimney, where they lodge more or less permanently. The trick is to be brave and get out where the chimney is wider. Where the chimney is wide enough to allow purchase with a foot on the front wall, the climbing is much easier. Rest by spanning the chimney between your back and foot. Move upward by pushing against the back wall with the other foot and one or both hands in order to lift your torso **(Figure 47).** Then bring the back foot forward to a position above the front foot and move the front foot back to begin the next cycle of lifting. Your feet move alternately forward and back. Your hands do the same, or both may push against the wall behind you.

In chimneys much wider than 3 feet you can no longer keep your back against one wall; the climbing becomes stemming (see **Figure 13**). The widest chimneys require both hands on one wall and both feet against the other. This is very strenuous.

All of the maneuvers just described can be used in dihedrals as well as chimneys.

Figure 47. Back and foot chimney technique used in a dihedral.

Resting

The difference between a good climber and a great one is the ability to *stop in a tough place* to rest, to work out the next moves, to place the needed protection. In part, this ability results from physical and mental conditioning. Knowledge of the techniques for resting and sheer ingenuity also come into play. I have mentioned ways of resting all along, but here is a brief summary of techniques:

1. Heel holds
2. Balancing on a straight leg
3. Stemming (probably the most useful technique)
4. Gripping the rock with thumbs, palms, hand hook, or fist (to rest fingers)
5. Hanging down on a straight arm
6. Foot or leg jams (often free hands)
7. Heel hooks (support weight on overhangs)
8. Back and foot chimney position (possible in corners as well as chimneys)
9. Crouching in hollows (to free hands)

In recent years I have adopted a somewhat unusual form of training. I do boulder problems as slowly as possible. I test how many places I can put one or both hands down at my sides. I lean far to the right and far to the left, stretch high, and crouch low on every hand- and foothold. It is a strange kind of adagio dance, but extraordinary conditioning and very instructive.

4

Ropes, Anchors, and Belays

When I was a very young climber, several encounters with British, French, and German climbers vividly impressed upon me the fact that Europeans and Americans had very different attitudes toward the employment of ropes, anchors, and belays. The Europeans seemed to think that the worst consequences of a fall were best avoided by not falling. The rope was used mainly for psychological support or for a less skilled second. Anchors were employed sparingly (or else for aid). Belays were probably not very effective. In the unlikely event of a fall, the worst *was* likely—and it was part of the game. Climbers occasionally got killed.

When American climbers took over European rope techniques in the 1930s, they quickly modified them to make them more effective. The Southern California climbers I knew in the 1950s deliberately pushed themselves to the limit. They insisted that belays work. A few of them fell fairly often; however, injuries were rare and fatalities unheard of.

Today the situation is much changed from the fifties. You should bear firmly in mind a few salient points:

1. Modern equipment and procedures for protection are highly efficient. This fact was brought home to me recently when I held two 35-foot leader falls in quick succession. Correctly employed, the system works very well. However, the climber who carries the usual gear is not necessarily safe.

2. Climbing standards have advanced greatly, so climbers routinely venture onto much more difficult terrain than in the past. Because competent instruction is relatively scarce, many of these climbers are not very skilled.

3. Consequently, injuries and fatalities have become commonplace. Most of these accidents involve inexpert climbers and result from obvious procedural errors. Expert climbers are rarely hurt making bold leads.

Rock climbing can be as safe as the individual climber wants to make it, provided he understands the hazards and respects the limitations of his equipment and of his own skills. To that end this chapter emphasizes basic principles of anchoring, belaying, protection, and so on, and for most climbing situations provides the outline of a single, versatile procedure. This approach reflects two philosophical biases: (1) Procedures with equipment should always be subordinate to skill in movement. In my view ropes and hardware are a necessary evil. (2) I dislike gear and methods which are complicated or specialized. I prefer the simple and versatile. I believe these biases are in the mainstream of American climbing tradition, with its emphasis on style.

Climbing Ropes

As the old adage goes, it is not the fall that hurts, it's the sudden stop. A stout rope that stops a falling leader suddenly may do him little good. His body may break under the impact, or the anchors may give way and the climber resume his flight. He may pull his companions down with him. Among early climbers the maxim was: The leader absolutely must not fall. Sometimes he even belayed his rope over a sharp edge of rock in the hope that it would break if he betrayed his trust.

In the thirties American climbers developed the *dynamic belay*. The falling leader was stopped gradually by the simple expedient of letting the belay rope slip through the second's hands. The dynamic belay required skill and was practiced assiduously with the help of pulleys and weights to simulate long falls.

In the fifties the Germans developed the dynamic rope, which stops the falling leader gradually by stretching. Rope stretch or elongation

absorbs much of the energy generated by the fall. The energy not absorbed by the rope is retained by the climber's body, and upon impact this energy is also transmitted to the anchors. Thus the crucial characteristic of climbing ropes is not absolute strength but rather *energy absorption capacity*. Other kinds of rope stretch, too, but under small loads. They have less energy absorption capacity. Ropes specially designed for climbing generally meet standards set by an international organization (Union Internationale des Associations d'Alpinisme) and are so labeled. Don't lead on any other kind of rope.

Climbing ropes have a distinctive *kernmantle* construction (a woven sheath over a braided core) which sets them apart from the more familiar laid, or twisted, ropes. The preferred length for climbing ropes is 50 meters (165 feet). Diameters range from 10 to 11 millimeters. An 8 or 9 millimeter rope is useful for hauling and rappelling but does not meet U.I.A.A. standards for holding falls unless it is used doubled.

Climbing ropes are extremely fragile. You must be continually alert to protect your rope from abrasions and cuts. Damage most commonly occurs when a climber is lowered on the rope or makes bounds down the cliff on a rappel. Then the rope may be pulled or stretched across rough rock or a sharp edge. You should learn to climb down rather than being lowered and to rappel smoothly. Sharp edges should be avoided, padded, or blunted.

At this point it may be well to talk about a dangerous tendency in the manufacture and promotion of climbing ropes. The different brands of ropes are promoted largely on the basis of their "handling" characteristics (mainly flexibility) and their ability to hold a number of U.I.A.A. standard test falls before breaking. Climbers like flexible ropes and tend to think that a nine-fall rope is superior to a five-fall rope. One manufacturer has gone so far as to claim sixteen falls for its rope.

The great preponderance of actual climbing falls (leader falls) are much less severe than the U.I.A.A. standard fall, and it is questionable whether there is any practical merit to a rope which will withstand sixteen standard falls. In the quest for flexibility and increased numbers of falls, manufacturers may have produced ropes which stretch too much and cut too easily. All that stretch and ease of handling will do the leader no good when he hits a ledge or when the rope severs. For all practical purposes a five-fall rope

Figure 48a. A top rope set up incorrectly so that it abrades on the rock.

Figure 48b. A top rope set up correctly.

may be safer than a nine-fall rope. There have been several fatal accidents to expert climbers where this question appears relevant. When I go shopping for a rope, I want the *toughest* rope I can find (likely to be the least flexible) that meets U.I.A.A. standards.

Most climbers know better than to step on a rope, as that grinds tiny fragments of rock (and sometimes glass) into it, but I am always surprised by the number of people who will throw a good rope down in the dirt and broken glass at a top-roping site. And how many will allow it to scrape over the rock when lowering a climber with a top rope. Experienced climbers set a top rope up very carefully to avoid abrasion, or else they use an old "junk" rope **(Figures 48a** and **48b).**

Prolonged exposure to sunlight or gasoline fumes, abrasion of the sheath, and repeated falls may dangerously weaken a rope. Dirty ropes should be laundered following the usual procedures for synthetic fabrics.

Tie-Ins and Harnesses

I have met more or less experienced climbers who did not know how to belay, to rappel, or even to tie in with no more equipment than a rope; they needed harnesses, artificial anchors, and carabiner brakes. I once saw the evacuation of an injured climber down a sixty-foot, low-angle cliff delayed for ten minutes while one of the rescuers fumbled with a harness and carabiner brake rappel. How much faster and easier it would have been to make a body rappel, requiring neither harness nor carabiners but only the rope.

Methods and gear are endlessly varied. Your basic repertoire should be built up from the methods which are simplest and the equipment which is most versatile. Complicated gear is not necessarily better or safer. It may not be handy when you need it. It offers more opportunities for equipment failure and human error. Its use is gen-

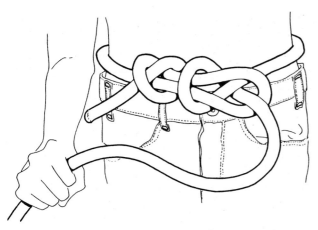

Figure 49. A tie-in with a bowline and overhand back-up.

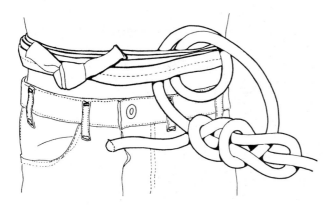

Figure 50. A tie-in to a swami belt.

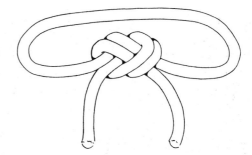

Figure 51. A ring bend.

erally time consuming. The ability to move fast is a virtue in climbing; in fact, it is the climber's primary protection from avalanches, bad weather, and untimely bivouacs. So start simple. Rely on simplicity whenever you can. Add more specialized gear and methods when you really need them.

Learn to attach yourself to the climbing rope, or *tie in*, first with a simple bowline around your waist backed up with an overhand knot around the waist loop **(Figure 49).** The back-up is necessary because rope is slippery. A bowline by itself may work loose while you are climbing. Even a bowline and back-up have been known to come loose. *These knots must be formed and tightened carefully.* Check them occasionally while you are climbing.

Many climbers think that a tie-in with a single loop of rope is painful, if not dangerous, in a fall. However, in the fifties Southern California

climbers pioneered many 5.9 routes and fell now and then with only a bowline around the waist. Most problems with tie-ins result from failure to locate them properly and make them snug. It is vitally important that the waist loop be at the narrowest part of your waist and as snug as possible without causing discomfort or cutting off air; otherwise, it will pull up over your ribs during a hard fall **(Figure 52a).** Climbers have broken ribs and punctured lungs that way.

The tie-in directly to the climbing rope has two drawbacks: (1) It uses up rope. (2) When the climber takes the rope off, for example, to set up a rappel, he is left without a ready means of anchoring himself to the cliff. For these reasons and for the supposed gains in comfort and safety, most climbers use a *swami belt* or a harness. A swami consists of four or five turns of rope around the waist separate from the climbing rope **(Figure 50).** One-inch tubular nylon webbing is preferred for this purpose. Alternatively, some climbers use a couple of turns of two-inch webbing.

The webbing is fastened with a ring bend **(Figure 51).** I use this simple, compact, reliable knot in most situations where two ends of rope are tied together. The knot must be formed and tightened carefully. To tighten it, grasp the knot in the palm of your hand and pull in turn each of the two ends and two ropes that emerge from the knot. Repeat this procedure several times. A swami should be just as snug around the waist as a bowline. Although it takes some trouble to achieve this, it is very important. A loose swami is dangerous.

Both the bowline and the swami are inadequate for situations where you must hang from your tie-in for more than a few seconds. Indeed, if you hang in space against your waist loop for more than a few minutes, there is real risk of suffocation. You should be lowered to a stance on the rock as quickly as possible. Or you may attach

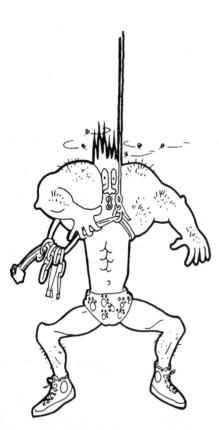

Figure 52a. This climber's waist loop wasn't snug at the narrowest part of his waist.

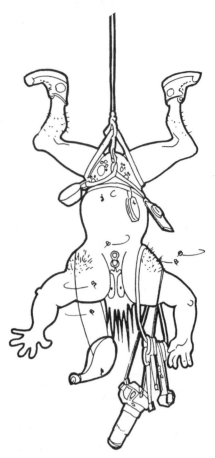

Figure 52b. This climber's point of suspension wasn't high enough on his body.

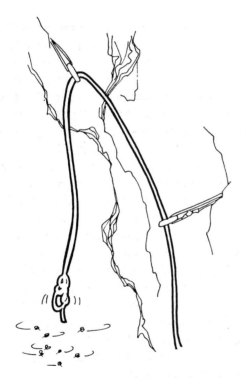

Figure 52c. This climber was attached to the rope with a carabiner.

Figure 52d. This climber pushed the tie-in knot around to his back.

Figure 52. Four potentially fatal errors with tie-ins.

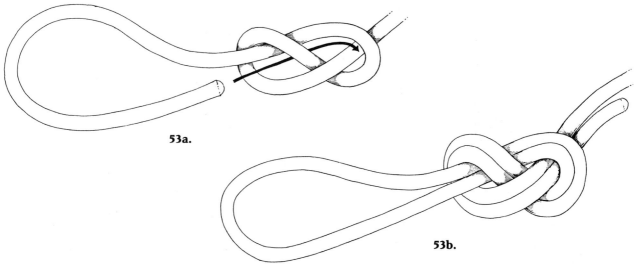

53a.

53b.

Figure 53. A figure-eight on a bight.

a runner to the rope above you with a prusik knot and assume the rest position on this improved stirrup (see Prusiking, Chapter 5). If this isn't possible, there is a quick and simple expedient: Swing your feet up over your head and hang upside down against your waist loop. There is a small risk that you will be unconscious from the impact of the fall, in which case you had better be wearing a *harness* or improvised seat.

Such situations used to be rare. They should still be extraordinary. However, climbers increasingly are tackling large overhangs. Some are "sieging" steep pitches, that is, falling or lowering down repeatedly in the process of working out the moves and fixing protection. In these cases some sort of seat is virtually necessary. Climbers also hang against the rope when rappelling. Harnesses are useful for this, but a seat is commonly improvised from runners (see The Carabiner Brake Rappel, Chapter 5). Harnesses are also useful for hanging belays, but many climbers carry an extremely lightweight and compact belay seat ("butt bag") or else improvise with runners, which will be discussed below.

A variety of harnesses are available or may be improvised, so generalizations are difficult. Most are cumbersome. Some are designed or may be used in a manner that causes a climber to flip sideways or backward in a fall, which has resulted in serious head and back injuries. It should be emphasized that a harness can be a very dangerous thing to fall against. It is vital that you be suspended from a point high enough on your body to keep you upright at the end of a fall **(Figure 52b)**.

I prefer a harness that comes in two pieces: a waist band and detachable leg loops. The leg loops can be stowed in your pack when not needed. They can also be used with an ordinary swami.

The climbing rope should always be tied directly around the swami or the material of the harness with a bowline or a figure-eight on a bight **(Figures 53a** and **53b)**. *Do not use a carabiner to attach the rope to your waist.* Deaths have resulted from this practice. The carabiner gate may open and the rope slip free during a tumbling fall. A locking carabiner avoids this hazard, but carabiners generally are weaker and less reliable than climbing ropes. Why interpose an unnecessary weak link at the most crucial point in your protection system? (See **Figure 52c**.)

Be sure that the tie-in knot is located directly at the front of your waist. Always keep it there. For this purpose I make an extra turn of the rope around my swami before tying the knot. Some climbers allow the knot to slide around to the side or deliberately push it around behind them. This will cause the climber's body to jackknife at the end of a fall, perhaps throwing his head against the rock **(Figure 52d)**.

Finally, some leaders allow their tie-in rope to pass downward between their legs. This is another good way to take a dangerous flip during a fall. Don't straddle the rope when you are leading; keep it to one side of your body.

The Basic Body Belay

A *belay* is any method that will check a falling climber by means of the rope. The simplest involves a companion, the belayer, who assumes a braced or anchored position above the climber, holds the rope tied to the climber, and takes in the slack rope.

Today, when so much climbing is done on steep walls with miniscule belay stances or hanging belays (where the belayer is actually supported by his anchors), the *belay anchor* seems all important. Many climbers are scarcely aware of the role which the configuration of the rock and the position of their own bodies play in an efficient belay. In the 1950s, when most climbers still thought of themselves as mountaineers, I was first taught to belay without any anchor. I learned to look for a stance where I could brace my legs or my whole body against a tug from the falling climber. I learned to anticipate exactly the direction that tug would come from, to take advantage of any little purchase the rock offered for butt or feet, and to position my body and the rope with exacting care. Later in tests I learned that a strong belayer well braced for a downward tug can support a load of about 400 pounds. Larger loads tend to pull the rope through his hands—okay, since that prevents him from being pulled out of position. Of course, an unanchored belay was used mainly in top roping, where the tug is seldom more than the climber's weight. I was taught to provide an anchor when it was needed. In most cases an anchor was needed for belaying the leader.

Today a stance is usually chosen where there is a handy anchor. Most climbers rely completely on the anchor and otherwise approach belaying pretty casually. Fortunately, belays are seldom put to a severe test, and in most cases an effective belay requires little skill. Still, the rather exacting practice of the old-fashioned body belay has a good deal of application in modern climbing.

First, on broken terrain there are often rock barriers or trees which offer a well-braced position and effectively take the place of an anchor. Time can be saved where an anchor is not needed or where a minimal anchor will serve, and on a long climb saving time is always a virtue. By the same token, equipment can be saved, which can be useful when gear is in short supply.

Second, belay anchors are sometimes unreliable. Even if the belayer has only a 2- or 3-inch ledge to stand on, his legs are braced against a downward tug, and *his body acts as a cushion between the anchor and the force of a fall*. In contrast, if he hangs against his anchor, the cushioning effect is minimized. The use of the belayer's body as a cushion to protect the belay anchor is one of the most important principles in belaying. I'll say more about it later.

Figure 54 illustrates the ideal body belay. Notice the following:

1. The belayer's feet are spread apart for lateral stability and braced in the likely direction of a tug. Her legs are straight, and her center of gravity is low (i.e., sitting is better than standing).

2. The rope from the climber passes between the belayer's feet, over one thigh, around behind her body, and then over the other thigh to her "holding hand." The location of the rope between her feet and over her thighs ensures that it cannot be ripped away from her body.

3. The friction of the rope passing snugly around her body and over her thighs makes it easy for the holding hand to check a fall. The belayer simply straightens her arm so that holding hand and arm are braced against her shoulder.

4. Both hands are used to feed out or haul in rope. It is important to coordinate them so that slack rope doesn't accumulate behind the belayer's back. And it is important to keep the holding hand on the rope *at all times* and in its place between the belayer's legs. This takes practice.

5. If only one leg can be braced well, the climber's rope should pass first around that side of the belayer so rope and braced leg are nearly parallel. Otherwise, she may be rotated out of her position.

6. As the belay rope passes around her body, it should lie just at the top of her hips. If it is higher on her back, she may be pivoted forward during a fall.

The body belay minimizes reliance on an anchor; nonetheless, in most cases an anchor will be needed. We'll cover anchors later in this chapter, but before learning to anchor you must understand the characteristics of various gear and the forces generated by a fall, which are treated next.

Figure 54. A body belay.

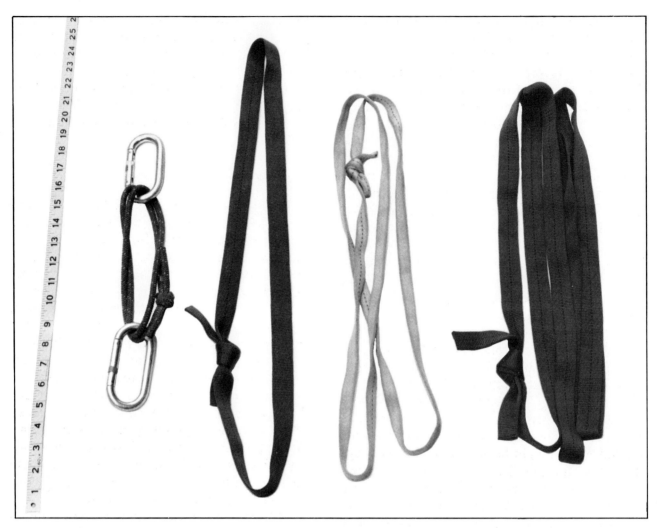

Figure 55. Runners. From left to right: a "quick draw," a standard runner, a thin runner for tying off knobs, and a long runner.

Runners

A *runner* is a short length of rope tied or sewn into a loop. I use the ring bend for tying runners and check the knots frequently since they will work loose when newly tied. Sewing avoids this problem, and, when properly done, it is supposed to be stronger. Nevertheless, I prefer the ring bend, which is a completely known quantity to me and which is easily untied and retied.

Runners are used for purposes too numerous to list here, but we'll encounter many of them in the sections that follow. For the ordinary run of climbing the leader may carry a dozen or more. The second should carry an assortment sufficient for prusiking.

Runners come in a variety of lengths and are made from diverse kinds of rope and webbing. In a general way the length of runners is determined by their use. Beyond that, my runners are sized

for convenience of transport over my shoulder (i.e., around the neck and one arm). A runner which is too short will be difficult to remove from around your neck; one which is too long will remove itself by sliding off your shoulder. Longer runners should fit well when doubled or tripled. I use five different lengths of runners, to which I have attached simple descriptive names (**Figure 55**):

1. *Standard runners.* Made from 5 feet of 1-inch tubular nylon webbing. Used variously, but mainly for rigging protection. I carry six to eight on most leads.

2. *Long runners.* Made from 11½ feet of 1-inch tubular webbing (too long for smaller people). Used mainly as a seat for rappelling and prusiking. Handy for rigging belays and tying off large blocks and trees. I carry one tripled over my shoulder. It is a little snug that way, but all

the more easily separated from the standard runners over the same shoulder.

3. *Thin runners.* Made from 8 feet of $^9/_{16}$-inch tubular nylon webbing. Used mainly for trying off knobs and horns of rock. Carried doubled over the shoulder. I carry one, more if the terrain has abundant knobs and horns.

4. *Short runners or "quick draws."* Made from 3½ feet of 7-millimeter kernmantle rope. Used mainly for rigging protection and for prusik knots. Carried on the climber's rack doubled with two carabiners attached. For rigging protection they are ordinarily used doubled. I carry two or more.

5. *Hero loops.* Made from 30 inches of $^9/_{16}$-inch tubular webbing. Used for tying off pitons (see Pitons) or threading the eye of a piton. The name originates from their use as a stirrup in aid climbing—standing up so high on an aid pin is a heroic effort. I carry one in a back pocket.

The strength of runners is close to or greater than that of most carabiners. In particular, the loop strength of 1-inch tubular webbing is about 4,000 pounds. However, webbing is especially subject to weakening by abrasion and prolonged exposure to sunlight because a large percentage of the fiber is exposed at the surface. Inspect your runners frequently. When in doubt, retire a runner to "junk" status. A runner which is no longer trustworthy for holding a leader fall may still be more than adequate for rigging a rappel.

Carabiners

Carabiners (also called *biners*) are aluminum alloy links with a gate which permits insertion of the climbing rope or a runner. They come in a variety of sizes and shapes. Most climbers use the standard oval carabiners for most purposes. Biners are used mainly for attaching the rope to anchors. The rope may be tied to a carabiner or may simply run through it.

There are a number of manufacturers, and quality control appears more difficult with biners than with ropes. Periodically one or another manufacturer will produce a bad lot. It is difficult to know a good biner when you see one. However, inspect the gate carefully. It should snap shut, and when open it shouldn't wobble on its attaching pin. The biner should appear fitted precisely and finished lovingly.

Like ropes, carabiners are fragile. Aluminum abrades and cuts easily and is notoriously subject to work hardening—that is, under repeated strains or blows the metal becomes brittle and breaks. Take care of your biners and inspect them often. Don't hammer on them, use them as a hammer, or drop them off cliffs, even low ones. Beware of the edges of bolt hangers. Under a load these will easily gouge the inside surface of a biner.

Anchors

An *anchor* is any means of attaching the rope to the cliff. It may be a tree, a heavy block of rock, a knob or horn of rock, a hole through the rock, or a stone securely wedged in a crack (i.e., a chockstone). Anchors provided by the terrain are called *natural anchors.* Alternatively, the climber may use any of a variety of mechanical anchors: chocks, pitons, and bolts. These *artificial anchors* require a crack or a hollow in the rock. Bolts are used where there isn't a naturally occurring crack or hollow and the climber must drill a hole.

Anchors which will withstand a pull in any direction are called *nondirectional anchors.* Those which withstand a pull only in one or more particular directions, such as downward and outward, are *directional anchors.* Trees, pitons, and bolts are usually nondirectional; knobs, horns, and chocks are commonly directional.

The location of one anchor often determines the direction of the pull on other anchors. This is seldom important with nondirectional anchors, but the use of directional anchors creates *protection systems* with interdependent parts. Properly placed, one anchor may help hold the others in place, but badly placed it may cause the others to pull out. The climber must be alert and mechanically savvy. Since natural anchors and chocks are the foundation of the modern clean climbing ethic, and their use requires a special set of skills, the beginner should devote a good deal of attention to directional anchors and protection systems.

Clean Climbing

Formerly climbers relied for anchors mainly on *pitons,* that is, metal spikes driven into cracks in the rock with a hammer. European climbers generally left the pitons in place for subsequent parties to use *(fixed pitons).* In America pitons were at first imported from Europe, and they were scarce. Later, Americans developed a superior piton made of steel alloy, but initially these were also scarce and too costly to leave behind. In any case, these alloy pitons were very tough—they could be driven and removed repeatedly during the climb. It wasn't necessary to carry a hundred or two hundred of them on a big wall climb, as was the practice in Europe; a selection of thirty would do. So Americans got into the habit of removing their pitons as they went along. Indeed, it was a point of honor to leave routes iron free for the greater challenge and enjoyment of subsequent parties.

Unfortunately, this idealistic attitude created a new problem. Outstanding routes became popular objectives and were climbed by as many as a hundred parties in a year, each party driving and removing its own pitons. The steel alloy pitons proved tougher than the rock. Inexorably the rock was gouged away, leaving conspicuous piton scars. In some cases a tight crack which originally accepted only the thinnest pitons became pockmarked with holes which made ample footholds. What was an aid climb became a man-made free climb **(Figure 56).** Or what was a challenging free climb became relatively easy.

To climbers a crack is a thing of beauty. Piton scars are an ugly intrusion worse even than the fixed iron. Fortunately, British climbers had already provided a solution to this problem. From the beginning many of the best British climbers steadfastly resisted the use of pitons. Instead, they relied on natural anchors, often chockstones. Sometimes they carried small stones along with them to wedge into cracks as needed. It was a small step from this practice to the use of machine nuts for the same purpose. Today the design of artificial chocks and other camming devices has become very sophisticated. Since these are inserted and removed with the climber's fingers rather than a hammer, there is practically no damage to the rock.

A whole ethic called *clean climbing* has grown up around the use of natural anchors and artificial chocks. The object is to conserve the climbers' environment in as pristine a state as possible so that countless subsequent parties may enjoy something like the beauty and adventure of the first ascent. The ultimate extension of this ethic is the growing practice of leaving no record of an ascent so that each party may discover a great route for itself.

Natural Anchors

How easily our vision is narrowed by our technology! I once saw an inexperienced leader fuss for twenty minutes at a belay stance trying to get a chock placement in a difficult crack when there was a perfectly good rock horn eighteen inches away from his shaky chock. Natural anchors are much more abundant than most climbers imagine, but you must cultivate the habit of looking for them. Sometimes you must deviate from your intended path in order to take advantage of a natural anchor. However, it is very satisfying to use natural anchors. A familiar, uninteresting route may appear new and challenging when you consider climbing it with only natural anchors.

Trees are the most obvious natural anchors. Even a very tiny tree trunk—perhaps only an inch or two in diameter—may make a strong anchor, though you should see a sturdy root penetrating into the rock and vigorous growth indicating live wood. Test trees vigorously by pulling on them with your hands. Avoid dead wood and shallow-rooted bushes. Dead wood becomes brittle, and dead trees lose their root systems to decay. I have seen quite large dead trees that a gentle shove would send down.

Bushes, of course, may be rooted only in "munge," the climber's term for dirt that adheres to cracks and ledges. Once in Yosemite two climbers were found dead at the base of a popular route with an uprooted bush attached to the rope between them.

Figure 56. Climbing pin scars; a manmade free climb.

Figure 57a. Anchoring the rope directly to a tree.

Figure 57b. Anchoring to the tree with a runner.

A belay can be anchored directly to a tree or branch with the climbing rope and a carabiner. If the tree is large, this uses a lot of rope. Alternatively, a runner may be looped around the tree and the rope tied to that with a carabiner. An overhand knot on a bight is used in either case **(Figures 57a** and **b)**. For a protection point the leader may simply place his rope behind a tree, that is, between the tree and the wall, being careful that it cannot jam there. However, it is usually worth the trouble to place a runner and carabiner on the tree.

The position of the rope or runner on the tree or branch will determine the leverage exerted. It is well if the rope is at the base of the limb and the leverage thus minimized. Keep firmly in mind that a branch may be torn off a tree by downward leverage. In general, a branch is not nearly as strong as a trunk of the same size.

A block of rock weighing several hundred pounds (roughly three times the size of a five-

gallon tin) and firmly seated on a ledge is an effective nondirectional anchor. A much smaller block will serve in a pinch as an anchor against an upward pull.

The strength of a rock knob or horn is difficult to judge, and even vigorous testing is unreliable. You can rule out a horn which moves, but you cannot rely on a horn because it feels firm. It is better to rely on careful visual inspection. Any crack or cleavage plane which penetrates the base of the horn or knob should make it suspect. A companion and I once climbed cautiously around a 3-foot-high, semidetached flake of rock which looked suspicious to us. Other climbers tried hard to pull it off and finally judged it safe. Nonetheless, it fell away the next day, seriously injuring one climber and nearly hitting several others. It's best to be conservative around large horns or flakes. Smaller pieces of rock will probably do less damage if they come away from the cliff.

Knobs and horns are often directional. Commonly a horn is good for a downward pull, but the upward drag of the rope as the leader climbs above it is often enough to remove the runner. The runner may be fastened around the horn so that it draws tight **(Figure 58).** It may be weighted in place by hanging surplus equipment from it. Or it may even be held in place with tape.

Finally, there are holes through the rock and natural chockstones through and around which runners may be threaded. Chockstones may be either directional or nondirectional. They should be inspected and tested. A chockstone may pull out if either the containing sides of the crack or the supporting edges of the stone crumble.

A runner can be simply looped around a chockstone, or it can be cinched tight around the *point of contact* between the chockstone and the containing rock so that it jams the stone into place. The chockstone in **Figure 59a** pulled outward easily. As rigged in **Figure 59b,** it provided a strong nondirectional anchor.

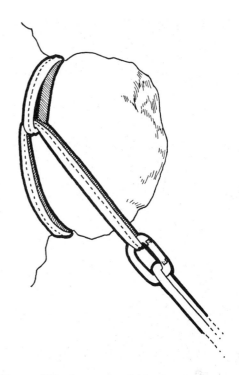

Figure 58. A runner cinched on a horn.

Figure 59a. A chockstone slung incorrectly.

Figure 59b. The same chockstone slung correctly.

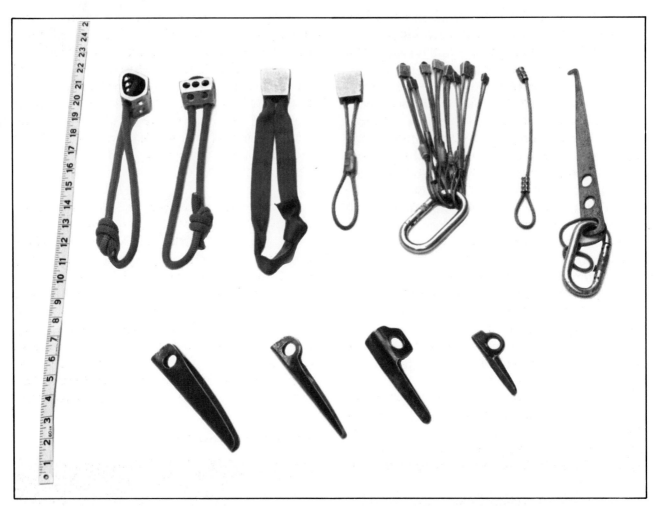

Figure 60. Chocks and pitons. *Top row, from left to right:* two hexentrics, two large stoppers, an assortment of tiny stoppers, a copperhead, and a chock pick. *Bottom row, from left to right:* two angle pitons and two horizontal pitons.

Chocks

The hammer firmly in hand, the ring of steel upon steel, the resistance of the rock as a piton was driven home all contributed to the leader's sense of security during the Golden Age of American rock climbing—the 1950s and 1960s. I well remember the first time I ventured onto a steep rock face without a hammer. I was repeating a familiar route, but with only chocks for protection. It was a whole new adventure. Many climbers had a tough time making the psychological adjustment to climbing with chocks. It was much easier for newcomers who had never got used to the seeming greater security of pitons.

Chocks are wedged into cracks and hollows in the rock with the climber's fingers. They were introduced into this country as a means to clean climbing. However, I am certain that chocks gained rapid acceptance for two other reasons: (1) They are more interesting and more fun to use than pitons. Many climbers are attracted to the mechanical intricacies of aid climbing; chocks add a similar dimension to free climbing. (2)

Chocks are often easier and quicker to place than pitons; thus they reduce the difficulty of protecting many pitches. When the 5.10 standard of difficulty (see Chapter 6) was introduced to Yosemite Valley in the early sixties (before chocks were available), many strenuous cracks were first free-climbed with minimal protection. Better to "lead on through and protect later" than risk a fall trying to drive a piton on such difficult terrain. Today climbers with less skill and daring than the pioneers are leading these same pitches and protecting them well with chocks.

There was skepticism at first, but chocks have greatly expanded the opportunities for protection. Often they provide solid placements in hollows and shallow cracks unsuitable for pitons. I have seen pitches completely unprotectable with pitons which are well protected with chocks.

Fixed pitons are still widely used, however, where chock placements are difficult or lacking.

Chocks are fitted with either a wire cable loop or a rope sling for attaching a carabiner and the climbing rope **(Figure 60).** Ordinarily the climber must supply his own rope slings. Some older climbing catalogs and manuals recommend slings which are longer than are commonly used today. Long slings cause chocks on the climber's rack to dangle down by her knees and occasionally insert themselves in cracks. My slings are made from about 3 feet of 7- or 8-millimeter kernmantle rope (preferably 8 mm., if it will fit). For chock sizes which require a smaller diameter rope than 7 millimeters, I prefer a wire cable. The rope is threaded through the chock and tied into a loop with a ring bend. Some authorities recommend a grapevine knot, but it is unnecessarily bulky. Sling knots (both ring bends and grapevine knots) have a nasty habit of working loose! I inspect mine frequently and occasionally tighten them with the help of pliers.

With larger chocks there is some advantage to slings which are a smaller diameter (i.e., 7 or 8 mm.) than the holes provided for them. If the sling slides easily through these holes, it will readily serve in a pinch as an improvised runner or prusik loop.

What are the relative merits of wire cables and rope slings? Rigid cables allow the climber to reach a few inches higher for a chock placement. The relatively thin cables also slip through tighter constrictions and thread smaller holes—no small advantage, since it may make the difference between good protection and none at all. On the other hand, the rigid cable acts as a lever, which may pry out the chock if there is a drag or tug on it. *Every wired protection chock requires a runner,* which is attached to the chock with a carabiner. A runner may be connected directly to a rope sling without a carabiner (inefficient practice, however, unless carabiners are in short supply), and with rope slings the runner may sometimes be dispensed with (see Rope Drag).

I trust a knot I have tied myself further than I trust the metal swage which fastens the cable loop on a wired chock (a simple matter—the knot is better known to me and more easily inspected). Thus in critical situations (e.g., belay anchors) I may trust one well-placed rope-slung chock where I would insist on two wired chocks. In general, my smaller chocks are wired, the larger ones slung with rope.

My own experience has been mainly with the *stoppers* and *hexentrics* (or "hexes") manufactured by Chouinard (see **Figure 60**). These have been especially popular at the granitic climbing areas in California. The discussion of chockcraft later in this chapter will be limited to these types of chocks. Other types have worked well for specific situations (e.g., *copperheads* in pin scars) and in other parts of the country.

Friends

Unless you carry a large selection of chocks, the right size may not be handy when you need it. Chocks do not work in every crack, especially if the size isn't exactly right. In any case, some effort may be required to get a good placement—not easy when you are hanging from a strenuous hand or finger jam. Climbers have long fantasized about a camming device which will go in easily and adapt automatically to a continuous range of crack sizes and shapes. At last the fantasy has been realized in the form of *friends* **(Figure 61),** which have been heralded as the biggest technical

Figure 61. A friend in a crack.

breakthrough since the nylon rope. Most climbers have been enthusiastic about friends and quick to replace their hexes with them. Friends have played a major role in the "advance" of climbing standards. They are a stunningly efficient means of protection.

That much said, I must also say that I have some trouble with friends. (It is hard to write this with a straight face! Most of my friends use friends.) Essentially, friends offend my sense of style. One of the most accomplished rock climbers and certainly the most innovative and influential of our time, Royal Robbins, has said: "'Style' is a slippery word, difficult to define. In rock climbing it refers to the methods and equipment used, and the degree of 'adventure' involved in the ascent." I think the key word here is *degree.* We are dealing not with absolutes but with subtle judgments. Nor are we dealing with ethical issues but simply a matter of personal preference.

Friends have been used in the pioneering of 5.12 routes, the current "frontier" in rock climbing. I can easily understand the appeal of friends in this context: Suddenly something seemingly impossible is within reach. I am not a 5.12 climber, so perhaps I should keep quiet. However, I cannot help wondering if we are deceiving ourselves, if we have not mistaken an advance in technology for an advance in skill and achievement. Have friends allowed climbers to advance into more adventurous and demanding worlds, or have they simply made a problem easier? Is 5.12 protected by friends really an advance over 5.11 protected by chocks or bolts? Is 5.12 protected by friends really an advance over prefixed protection? There are, of course, no simple answers.

The most obvious answer is that "advance" is irrelevant. Climbers are responding to their own personal goals or just doing what they enjoy. I hope so, but when I read the climbing magazines and listen to the talk around climbing areas, this answer seems to me more rationalization than reality.

Among the arguments originally made in favor of chocks over pitons is that the former require a greater sensitivity to the qualities of the terrain and that they make protection a mental exercise rather than a power game. In these respects friends are a step backward in the direction of pitons. They require less sensitivity and skill. I hope that you will perfect your chock placement skills before you get the habit of friends.

A word of caution about friends: Their ability to work their way farther into a crack and thus become permanently lodged there is well known. An increasing number of routes now sport "fixed" friends, which were by no means left behind on purpose. Apart from the financial loss to the climber, fixed friends are especially offensive on classic routes long done without friends (for example, the East Buttress of Middle Cathedral Rock in Yosemite). The problems of fixed pitons and chocks are bad enough without adding friends to the list. Friends can also work their way out of a crack.

Pitons

Chocks are ordinarily removed by the climbing party as it proceeds. Pitons, or "pins", **(Figure 60)** are ordinarily left in place or "fixed" because the clean climbing ethic requires it. A thorough approach to clean climbing would dispense with pitons altogether. The usual justification for fixed pins is that they are necessary for reasonable protection where chock placements are lacking. In actuality, not only are most fixed pins unnecessary, they are unreliable. Most climbing parties do not carry a hammer, so fixed pins cannot be tested reliably. And parties that do carry a hammer often test a piton by pounding the head back and forth, which weakens the head. I estimate that fully half of the fixed pins on free climbs in Yosemite Valley have either an eye that is cracked or a head missing altogether. Often these useless pins obstruct perfectly good chock placements.

A good case can be made for fixed pins where two conditions are met: (1) Chock placements are in fact inadequate. (2) Someone will assume responsibility for the maintenance of the fixed pitons (the local climbing school?). These determinations should be made by a consensus of the leading climbers at a popular area.

If you use a fixed pin, you should:

1. Inspect the pin visually for cracks and rust. Severe bends are also suspect.

2. Inspect the placement visually. Ideally, the pin should make a right or an acute angle with the direction of the force likely to be exerted on it.

3. Test the placement with your fingers. (I assume that you are not carrying a hammer.) A loose piton is unreliable unless the angle of placement is especially favorable. However, even a tight piton may not be reliable.

Figure 62. A piton tied off with a hero loop.

4. If you have any doubt about the piton's soundness, back it up with a nearby chock placement.

A piton which is not fully driven may be "tied off" with a hero loop **(Figure 62).** This reduces the leverage exerted on the piton under the impact of a fall.

I hope that beginners will avoid the piton habit from the start. I would like to see pitons (and bolts) eliminated from *wilderness* climbing areas and also from aid climbing. The elimination of pitons would go a long way toward restoring the faded beauty and diminished challenge of climbs like the popular routes on El Capitan. People who insist on getting up things will not appreciate these suggestions. However, if nothing else, future generations will thank us for leaving some rock clean.

Bolts

While pitons have become less acceptable in recent years, *bolts* have found increasing acceptance. There was a time and place where bolts

definitely were not acceptable. In Southern California in the 1950s, bolts were practically unthinkable. There was only one bolt on a major route at Tahquitz Rock and that had been placed years earlier. Then a climber came from another area and placed two bolts on two of the most outstanding pitches at Tahquitz. One of these bolts, while protecting the leader, posed a serious hazard to the second: If he fell off the crux move, he would be dangling in space with no convenient place to lower to. The bolt was summarily "chopped." The other bolt protected an 80-foot jamcrack which traditionally had been led fourth class, or without protection. The pitch, while not difficult, was a real test of a leader. The local climbers argued over that bolt for many hours before it was removed. They didn't want it there, but they faced the prospect of an inept leader taking a fall if they removed it. Their attitude seems strange today, when bolts appear and disappear on popular routes with casual regularity, but it was in part responsible for the revolution in free-climbing standards which occurred at Tahquitz in the early fifties. Style was important even in matters of protection.

Today many climbers take it upon themselves to place bolts on long-established and popular routes where countless parties, often of modest abilities, have managed quite well without bolts. Often these climbers don't know how to place a bolt properly (or how to locate it properly). Snake Dike on Half Dome in Yosemite is perhaps the most famous example of this abuse. This route, which is of very modest difficulty (one 5.7 move), was first climbed without bolts. It was beautiful and challenging before it was thoroughly bolted, then littered with chopped studs, then bolted again.

It is easy to argue that Snake Dike wasn't safe without bolts. Certainly it wasn't safe for beginners. But does anyone propose to make *every* climb safe for beginners? Does anyone seriously believe that there will be fewer accidents if only there are more bolts?

On the other hand, there are a few arrogant climbers who attempt to keep the rest of the world below their own lofty level by chopping long-established bolts or simply stealing the hangers. The problem of hanger theft is so widespread that I have started carrying one or two hangers on my rack.

Climbers will argue over these matters *ad nauseum*. The point is that routes are specific en-

Figure 63. A quarter-inch Rawldrive bolt and hanger.

tities which have a history and often a special meaning for the climbers who do them. The customs and standards in each climbing area serve useful purposes and play a role in the evolution of climbing. Local practices deserve respectful consideration, and one bolt more or less does alter a route.

The great thing about bolts is that they have opened up a whole class of splendid routes which cannot be protected with chocks or pitons, routes on nearly featureless faces between crack systems. The Glacier Point Apron in Yosemite is perhaps the best-known area for bolt-protected face climbs. Suicide Rock and Joshua Tree National Monument in Southern California offer distinguished examples of the genre. In nearly all cases the bolts were placed on the lead, in accordance with the prevailing ethic, so the first ascents were especially bold and skillful enterprises. Subsequent parties have had a relatively easy time of it.

There are a great variety of bolts in use, and in general the bolts used by climbers have not been designed or manufactured for climbing. From time to time the manufacturers express consternation that climbers would entrust their lives to bolts. The bolt in most common use consists of a single quarter-inch diameter stud 1 or 1½ inches long **(Figure 63)**. While some of these bolts have held repeated falls, others apparently identical have failed under a climber's weight. Quality control in the manufacture of bolts is not as rigorous as that expected with other climbing gear, and visual inspection is of little use.

Climbers commonly rely on bolts which have been in place twenty years or more and which may have held severe falls. In some areas

old bolts are being systematically replaced by heavier and more secure types. This effort should be encouraged.

You should certainly not expect a bolt to hold a severe fall. For belay and rappel anchors the prevailing practice is two bolts, preferably of different manufacture since two bolts from the same batch may be similarly defective. It is a brave (foolish?) party that will commit itself to a single bolt at a belay stance or rappel anchor. I want two bolts which appear in all respects reliable. Even then I am nervous and make every effort to avoid putting those bolts to a severe test.

Bolt technology is complex, and there are relatively few masters of the art of correct bolt placement. Both subjects are beyond the scope of this book. The beginner need merely recognize that *bolts are always of dubious reliability*. If you did not place the bolt, you do not know its history. The bolt hole may be too large or shallow. The bolt may have been weakened by weathering or falls. None of these conditions is reliably determined by visual inspection. I offer the following advice:

1. Do not place or chop bolts unless you have made a thorough study of the matter. This will require extended discussions with expert climbers. Otherwise, you will be creating a snare for other naïve climbers.

2. Do not trust a bolt which is bent or incompletely driven.

3. Inspect the hanger for rust or cracks. Look especially for hairline cracks adjacent to the hole that fits the stud.

4. Beware of aluminum hangers. Aluminum is notoriously subject to work-hardening. Many old aluminum hangers which have been ham-

mered on, fallen on, or aided on repeatedly have become brittle and finally broken under small loads.

5. If the hanger is attached by a nut, be sure that the nut is tight. Be sure that the stud is not inclined so that the force of a fall or the load of a rappelling climber may strip the threads.

6. Test bolts with your fingers, but please don't hammer on them. Hammering on a bolt never accomplishes anything except weakening the bolt.

7. For belay or rappel anchors insist on *two bolts* or else back up with chocks or other anchors.

Tying into the Anchor

On steep rock, unless you are belayed, you should be tied into an anchor. There are just too many ways to fall or get knocked off even a comfortable ledge. Usually you can tie in with the climbing rope. Make an overhand knot on a bight and clip this into the anchor with a carabiner. Alternatively, you may attach yourself to the anchor with a runner, thus leaving the climbing rope free.

Many climbers attach the runner to their waist with a carabiner. This is just as dangerous as tying into the climbing rope with a carabiner. If you tumble or are twisted around, the biner at your waist may snap free. You should loop the runner around your waist band and through itself. Or you may use two biners with opposed gates. Of course, the same hazard arises in anchoring a belay. Beware of the biner at your waist.

Principles of Belaying and Protection

Throughout the 1950s and 1960s rock-climbing fatalities were rare in the United States. Certainly there were many fewer climbers than today, but climbers were constantly pushing the boat out into more adventurous and seemingly more dangerous waters. Both free climbing and big wall climbing advanced impressively in the sixties. Occasionally a leader was hurt in a fall; however, one kind of accident was almost unheard of: a fall which carried all the members of a climbing party to the ground. I remember thinking at the time that such an accident was virtually impossible given the prevailing methods of belaying. In Europe that kind of accident was commonplace, but it could not happen in the United States.

Without checking the record I can recall three such accidents in Yosemite Valley alone in recent years. Each of these was a clear case of failure to recognize the mechanical limitations of equipment and the forces that can be generated by even a very short fall—perhaps *especially* by a very short fall—or even by simply hanging against the rope.

Climbers who would be safe must be mechanically savvy. They must understand that a bolt or a carabiner may withstand a large load applied in one direction but break if the same load is applied in another direction. They must recognize that a twenty-foot fall may generate small forces in one situation and very large forces in another. They must be sensitive to "little" details of procedures with rope and gear because these details may make the difference between life and death, determining, for example, whether a falling leader hits a ledge or is stopped a foot short of it.

In the following sections I will outline the mechanical principles which underlie the modern practice of belaying and protection. I will describe basic procedures which cover most situations. You will learn other ways from other climbers, but more important than specific procedures is the habit of thinking mechanically in every situation: What directions will the forces come from? How large will they be? Exactly how will they hit each link in the chain of gear? Is each link adequate to its particular task? And what will happen should a link fail?

The Forces Generated by a Fall

A falling climber gathers energy as long as he gathers speed. When the rope slows his descent, this energy is absorbed by the deformation of his body, by the stretching of the climbing rope, by the friction of the rope sliding over carabiners and perhaps through the belayer's hands, and by the movement of the belayer and perhaps some of the anchors. Rope stretch and slide are desirable as long as the climber doesn't hit anything and the rope doesn't cut on a sharp edge. Within narrow limits movement of the belayer is OK, even desirable. Movement (i.e., failure) of anchors is inevitably frightening, if not downright dangerous!

Energy absorption may occur suddenly over a small distance (i.e., very little rope stretch), in which case the forces generated are relatively large. Equipment and bodies may break or pull

Table 1. Forces Generated by Hypothetical Falls (K = 2)

Distance above protection	$X^{acceleration}$	$X^{deceleration}$	Total fall	Climber's weight	Force on climber
10 ft.	20 ft.	10 ft.	30 ft.	150 lbs.	750 lbs.
10 ft.	20 ft.	5 ft.	25 ft.	150 lbs.	1,350 lbs.
10 ft.	20 ft.	2 ft.	22 ft.	150 lbs.	3,150 lbs.
20 ft.	40 ft.	10 ft.	50 ft.	150 lbs.	1,350 lbs.
40 ft.	80 ft.	20 ft.	100 ft.	150 lbs.	1,350 lbs.

away from the rock. Or energy absorption may happen more gradually over a larger distance, in which case the forces are relatively small. The force on the climber's body can be estimated as follows:

$$F = W \cdot K \cdot \frac{X^{acceleration}}{X^{deceleration}} + W$$

where *W* is the climber's weight, *K* is a "fudge factor" ranging in value from about 1 to 2, $X^{acceleration}$ is the distance over which the falling climber gathers speed, and $X^{deceleration}$ is the distance over which he slows to a stop. The value of *K* depends on whether energy absorption is mainly by sliding friction (about 1) or rope stretch (2).

Table 1 shows the forces computed for a few hypothetical falls using the most extreme case (*K* = 2). Notice that, as long as the climber doesn't hit anything, the shortest fall in the table generates the largest force. Of course, the farther a climber falls, the *more likely* he is to hit something and hit it hard. Obviously, $X^{deceleration}$ is the critical factor. In most actual falls with modern equipment and methods, $X^{deceleration}$ is determined mainly by the absolute amount of rope stretch. Five feet of stretch is better than two feet (as long as the climber doesn't hit anything). Climbing ropes are made to stretch and thus keep the peak load well below the largest force in Table 1.

However, *the absolute amount of stretch depends on the length of rope available to stretch,* that is, on the length of rope paid out between the climber and the belayer. The most critical time is the time

before the leader clips into the first protection above the belayer. Then $X^{acceleration}$ will be twice the length of rope paid out and $X^{deceleration}$ (from rope stretch) will be relatively small. Toward the end of a long lead, assuming the leader has protected it, the same $X^{acceleration}$ (say, for a 20-foot fall) will be more like one-sixth or one-seventh the length of rope paid out, and $X^{deceleration}$ will be relatively large. Other things being equal, a 20-foot fall at the beginning of a lead will generate larger forces than a 20-foot fall at the end of the lead.

However, other things are not equal. It is the belayer who applies the brakes, and there is a limit to how large a force he can withstand before the rope begins to slide through his hands, assuming a body belay. Above this limit—about 400 lbs. (at the belayer) for a strong belayer—the belay is automatically a dynamic one. This limit is reached in situations where energy absorption by rope stretch and by intermediate protection anchors is minimal, that is, early in the lead, and most of the energy of the fall is transmitted to the belayer.

It should be kept clearly in mind that the 400-pound force cited above is an upper limit *at the belayer.* As it is transmitted along the rope toward the climber this force is multiplied by frictional resistance of the rope binding over rock and carabiners. The forces generated by a fall act in either direction along the rope. In the following section I will trace them from the falling climber toward the belayer.

750 LB + 400 LB = 1150 LB

Figure 64. The addition of forces in a fall.

The Transmission and Addition of Forces in a Fall

The force on the falling climber is transmitted undiminished (except by frictional resistance, usually very small) along the rope to the nearest (i.e., usually the highest) anchor. Thus a 750-pound tug on the climber is also a 750-pound tug on the anchor. There is another tug on that anchor, the tug from the rope which leads down to the belayer. These two forces must be added together to get the total load on the anchor. The tug from the belayer's end of the rope is less than that from the climber by the amount of frictional resistance as the rope binds over the carabiner at the anchor. For example, if the tug on the belayer's side of the anchor is 400 pounds, the total load on the anchor is 1,150 pounds (see **Figure 64**).

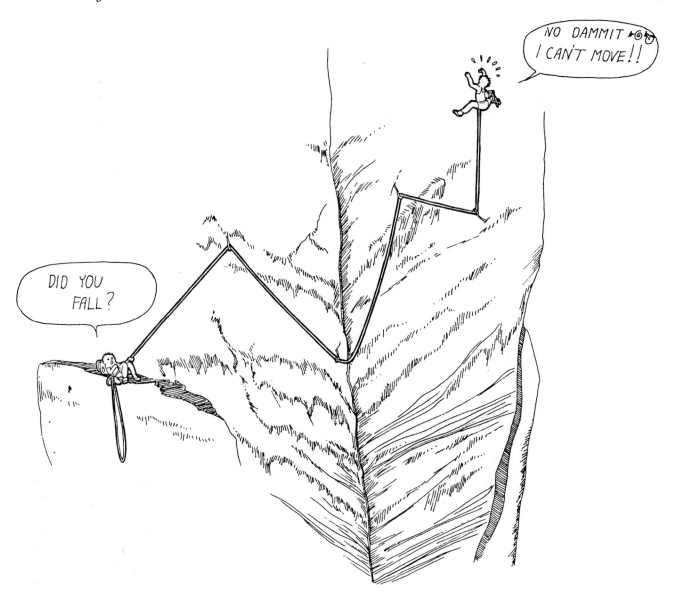

Figure 65. An inept leader stopped by rope drag.

The 400-pound force is transmitted along the rope to the next anchor, or, if there aren't any other anchors, directly to the belayer. The more protection points that the rope binds over, the more the forces generated by the fall are diminished by friction as they are transmitted from the falling climber toward the belayer.

Unfortunately, the same friction in the system which makes the belayer's job easier makes things difficult for the leader. "Rope drag" impedes the leader's movements rather like carrying a heavy pack up the rock. It may stop him altogether or precipitate a fall **(Figure 65).** It may lift runners off horns and chocks out of cracks. In a fall it reduces the effective length of the rope and thus its energy absorption capacity. The leader must be very careful to keep rope drag to a minimum, though this means the maximum force is transmitted to the belayer in a fall.

The Belay Anchor

The finish of a long, well-protected lead is the most secure time on a steep wall. The leader is a hundred feet or more above his belayer. That length of rope out represents an enormous energy absorption capacity. There are perhaps eight or a dozen protection points. If several of them fail, there are still many anchors attaching the climbers to the wall. In the event of a fall the force transmitted to the belayer will be small. He will be dragged upward, which is a very efficient means of energy absorption. His belay anchor is not likely to fail, but even if it does, the consequences are not serious. He need merely keep a hold on the rope as he is lifted upward a foot or two.

Conversely, *the beginning (or the changing) of the lead is the least secure time.* If it is a hanging belay, two climbers and a heavy haul bag may actually be supported by a small number of anchors. The energy absorption capacity of the system is at a minimum. If the leader should fall before he places his first protection, or if that anchor should fail, he will fall directly against his belayer. The tug will be downward, perhaps adding the belayer's own weight to the total load on the belay anchors. Such a downward tug, while a rare occurrence, is likely to be both more severe and more serious than an upward tug. Should the anchors fail, the worst will result.

These circumstances have several practical consequences:

1. When chocks, fixed pins, or bolts are used at a belay stance, most climbers insist on *at least two strong anchors against a downward tug.* If it is a stout tree, horn, or chockstone, or if the climber has driven a solid piton himself, a single anchor point may suffice. If the anchors are nondirectional, then an *upward* tug is provided for. In the case of chocks it is usually necessary to set a chock specifically for an upward tug. This chock, of course, should be located *below* any chocks set for a downward tug. Thus it takes three chocks to make a belay anchor. Occasionally, if I am ensconced on a big ledge or if there is an unusually good placement, I will make do with only two chocks.

2. The several chocks, fixed pins, and so on involved in a belay anchor should be tied together snugly with carabiners and/or runners, so that they hold one another in place. This is especially important with directional anchors. The belayer's rope is then tied to the combination. Occasionally

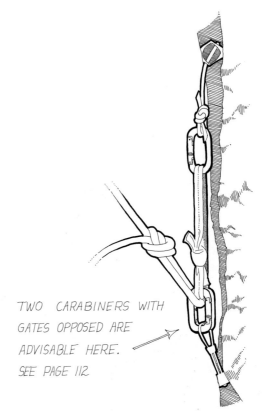

TWO CARABINERS WITH GATES OPPOSED ARE ADVISABLE HERE. SEE PAGE 112

Figure 66. A tie-in to belay anchors.

this procedure will be impractical, and the belayer will tie into several anchors separately (**Figures 66** and **67**).

3. The ideal location for a belay anchor (more precisely, for the tie into the combination of anchors) is a foot or two above the belayer's tie-in (i.e., his waist). If he is dragged upward by the force of a fall, so much the better. That is a good way to absorb the energy of the fall and protect the belay anchor. Being dragged upward is certainly preferable to being jerked downward off the stance.

4. Occasionally there will be no good anchor against an upward tug. In this case the anchors for a downward tug should be located as high as practical. If they are above the belayer's head, it is unlikely that he will be dragged upward the six feet or more that would be necessary before he is dragged against them.

5. Occasionally the leader will run out of rope a little short of a good belay stance. Assuming the lead is reasonably protected, the belayer should simply unanchor and begin climbing. The leader can then continue to a stance. It is only necessary for the two climbers to move more or less together so that a lot of slack rope doesn't accumulate between them.

6. By the same token, two climbers can move simultaneously rather than consecutively. The leader places protection at the front end of the rope as fast as the second removes it at the tail end. This procedure will seem a little unorthodox to many climbers, but where belay anchors are unreliable, it is a reasonable way to avoid committing both climbers to a bad anchor. It can also save a lot of time.

7. If there isn't a reliable belay anchor, there are several options. If the leader has enough rope, he can proceed to the next solid protection anchor, clip into that, and then climb back to a stance. If he hasn't enough rope, he can bring the belayer part way up the pitch, then proceed to a better stance. Or both climbers can move simultaneously. The important thing is to keep several sound anchors between the two climbers.

8. It is more important to protect early in a lead than later. As we have seen, the most serious fall is a long fall directly against the belayer. On hard rock I usually want two solid protection anchors in the first twenty feet of the lead.

9. It is common and dangerous practice in Europe to clip the leader's rope directly to the belay anchor, so that it also serves as the first protection. Thus the anchor is effectively located between the climber and the belayer. The force of a fall will hit the belay anchor before it hits the belayer. *This practice may as much as double the load on the anchor.* It is sounder practice to place a separate protection anchor as early as possible in the lead.

The same problem arises with hanging belays, where the leader must choose between clipping his rope into the anchor or risking a fall directly against the belayer. It would be nice if belay anchors were bombproof, but the two quarter-inch studs found at many hanging belays hardly qualify. A hanging belay should be located where protection is available immediately above or where the climbing to the first protection is relatively easy. Otherwise, a leader at all doubtful of the soundness of his anchor should consider one of the options in (7) above.

10. Sustained, hard rock right off the ground or a large ledge presents one of the most demanding situations in climbing. The most impressive jobs of leading I have ever seen have been twenty or thirty feet off the ground, where the leader placed protection at close intervals in order to prevent a possible groundfall—not easy on hard terrain. It is common practice to not anchor the belayer in such a situation, partly because the leader can't fall past him and partly because, without an anchor, the belayer may be able to take up some of the slack rope during a fall. One method of taking up rope is simply to run away from the leader. A more effective method is to spin around quickly on one foot, thus winding the rope around the belayer's body. If the belay rope is attached to the belayer correctly (see The Belayer), it won't matter which way he spins. However, if the leader is much heavier than the belayer, it is probably best to anchor the belayer snugly and to forget about trying to take up rope.

The Belayer

When the belayer is located between the force of a fall and the belay anchor, he serves as a cushion protecting the anchor and, as we have already seen, as a kind of safety valve; there is a limit to how tightly he can hold onto the rope. In the case of an upward tug the load on the belay anchor cannot much exceed the belayer's weight. In the case of a downward tug the load on the anchor may be as much as four times his weight.

In that worst case, where the climber falls directly against the belayer, it is the belayer who is in danger of injury (before the falling climber) and of losing control of the rope. He will want the best possible stance, braced in the direction of the tug (see The Basic Body Belay), and will need a tenacious grip on the rope. Few belayers wear gloves, perhaps because the worst case is (or should be) rare.

Many belayers use a *Sticht belay plate* (see Glossary) as a mechanical aid in holding onto the rope. However, this practice eliminates the safety valve function of the belayer and may also result in a harder belay. The forces generated by a fall and transmitted to the belay anchor may be greatly increased. Nonetheless, a Sticht plate is advisable if the belayer is much lighter than the climber. Especially strong anchors are also advisable in this case.

Today most belayers simply tie into an anchor, pass the climber's rope around their waist, and hold tightly to it. The old-fashioned, deliberate dynamic belay is considered obsolete. With

Figure 67. A belay on a minimal stance.

Figure 68. Use of a carabiner to hold the rope in position on the belayer's body.

modern ropes the prevailing practice is to hold on as tightly as possible. The resulting belay will be hard (climber stopped abruptly) or soft depending on the length of rope out, the friction or drag in the protection system, the cushioning effect of the belayer's body, and the amount of rope which *perforce* slips through his hands. This leaves a lot to chance.

I have already emphasized that belays are seldom put to a severe test and that the system is very efficient. When a falling leader is injured, it is rarely because the belay "failed." Rather, it is usually because the leader hit something on the way down, probably the belay ledge or the ground. Often he "grounded out" because a protection anchor "pulled." The belayer might possibly have helped matters by bringing the leader to a stop *more quickly,* so that he didn't hit anything. Or by bringing him to a stop *less quickly,* so

that the protection didn't fail. This dilemma is fairly common (especially on the first pitch of a climb), but few belayers give any thought to the subtleties of it. And fewer are ever blamed if the leader should fall and ground out. It may sound like a good problem for a computer, but I believe an experienced and alert belayer can judge the need for a hard or a soft belay and respond in a variety of ways.

The climber's rope passes around the belayer's waist *above* the tie into the belay anchor. Otherwise it may be pulled up directly against the anchor rope during an upward tug. It is held securely in place by a carabiner clipped to it and to the front of the belayer's swami belt or harness. During a fall this carabiner will tend to slide along the swami to the belayer's side or back. This is easily prevented if the biner is positioned so that it is held in place by the belayer's tie-in knot, which should also be at his front. *The carabiner will be on the same side of the knot as the belayer's holding hand* **(Figure 68).**

Belayers usually face toward the rock or sideways to it (toward the leader, if he is to one side). The sideways position allows the belayer to both watch the leader and enjoy the surrounding scenery. It also allows him to brace a leg against a downward tug. However, where practical, I prefer to face outward from the rock and brace both legs. If the belayer is sideways to the rock or if the lead goes to one side, the rope passing around his waist will tend to rotate him during a fall. He will be pulled around, either face toward the rock or face outward, depending on which way the rope passes around his waist. Some authorities say the rope should be arranged to turn him face toward the rock. I think it makes little difference except that one way will usually make for easier rope handling than the other. What is important is the position of the carabiner securing the climber's rope to the belayer's waist—rope handling will be easier if the rope doesn't make a sharp bend through it.

Apart from being ready to hold a fall, the belayer has several responsibilities:

1. First, in belaying the climber *up* to the belay stance, the rope should be collected neatly at the stance, free of tangles and ready to pay out on the next lead. Coils should be avoided. The rope can be looped back and forth on the belay ledge or, if there is no ledge, over the belayer's thigh or foot or anything at all so that it does not hang down the wall. Don't let it hang down the wall, unless there is no possibility of a loop of rope hanging up on anything down there. The only time I was nearly killed on a climb the party climbing above me had allowed their rope to hang down the wall. A loop caught around a large chockstone. When they pulled the rope free, the chockstone came loose and nicked my elbow as it sped down the wall; it might as easily have been my head. That was more than twenty years ago. I still have the scar as a reminder of how climbing accidents happen.

2. It is part of the belayer's job to keep the rope free of tangles and to pay it out as quickly as the leader needs it. Few things are more disconcerting to a leader than starting into a delicate or a strenuous move and suddenly being jerked back by the rope. The belayer should keep about a foot of slack in the rope in front of him and have one eye on it. As quickly as this rope inches upward, he should feed more rope around his waist. With practice this response becomes au-

tomatic. Some belayers avoid the need for a quick response by keeping three or four feet of slack in the belay rope. As a result the leader may suddenly fall farther than expected. The fine art of belaying consists of keeping excess slack out of the rope and still never permitting a tug on the leader.

3. The middle of the rope should be marked. When the mark passes through the belayer's hands, he should call "half the rope." The leader can then look back to see how far he has come, look ahead, and judge how far he can go. The belayer should also signal "twenty feet" and "ten feet" as the leader approaches the end of the rope.

Climbing Signals

Beginners are customarily taught a set of verbal signals which bear little relation to climbing realities. By venerable tradition the climber exchanges signals with his belayer before he starts to climb something like this:

On belay?
Belay on.
Climbing.
Climb!

This exchange is supposed to be an important safeguard. However, if climber and belayer are next to one another, it hardly seems necessary. Presumably both are alert and can see the situation. If climber and belayer are 150 feet apart on the wall and the wind is blowing, the signals can't be heard anyway or are easily subject to confusion. In this situation some climbers resort to a system of tugs on the rope, which are also easily subject to error, as tugs may occur anyway. The best signal is simply a predictable and failsafe procedure.

At the end of a lead, as soon as he is secure, the leader yells *off belay!* This signal is a time-saving device rather than a necessity. While the leader is completing his anchor and getting ready to belay, the climber below can prepare to climb. Ordinarily that climber will not complete the removal of his belay anchor until the leader has indicated his readiness by hauling up all the slack rope. Then the climber below moves up as long as the leader continues to haul up slack rope.

Other useful signals are:

Slack. This indicates that the climber needs more rope in order to maneuver. The belayer should pay out rope as the climber seems to require it. The leader should seldom need to use this signal since the belayer is paying out rope as needed anyway. Occasionally the leader will need a lot of rope quickly in order to clip into protection high above his head. Then it is helpful if he signals "slack."

Rope. Used mainly by the second (who climbs toward his belayer, while the leader moves away from his). This indicates either that the climber is nervous or that the belayer is asleep and has neglected to haul in rope. The belayer should take in rope.

Climbing. If the climber has stopped for a while to place or remove protection or to contemplate a hard move, it is helpful if he signals when he is climbing again.

Watch me. This indicates that the prospect of a fall has crossed the climber's mind. The belayer should be particularly attentive.

Rock! This signal is obligatory. If a rock dislodges, this should be yelled as quickly and loudly as possible: **ROCK!** Increasingly it is also needed for the haul bags, hardware, and other debris wall climbers drop on hapless souls down below. There is a certain irony involved in this use of "rock," but it is a warning every climber understands and responds to.

Signals of dubious value are:

Tension. Used by climbers who want to lean against the rope, this means that the belayer should haul up rope and hold tight. This is a very bad habit to get into, but may occasionally be necessary in order to remove a recalcitrant chock when you are in a difficult position.

Falling! This is a self-fulfilling prophecy and another very bad habit. If climbers never use this signal, there will be fewer falls.

A Philosophy of Protection

The free solo climber has dispensed with protection. Yet other skilled climbers (indeed some of the best) do not like to advance much more than ten feet beyond their last protection. And between the free soloer and the zealous protectionist are many gradations. The tendency among skilled climbers seems to be toward using less and less protection, that is, approaching free soloing by degrees. Personally, I am inclined to the position of those early-day alpinists who would unrope on terrain where sound anchors were lacking. When climbers rope together, I believe they should use the rope effectively. Ordinarily that

means placing a number of anchors which will stay placed in the event of a fall.

Relatively few individual anchors are "bombproof." A stout tree, a secure chockstone, or a piton the climber himself has driven may fit into that category. Bolts, fixed pins, and chocks ordinarily do not. The leader who "runs it out" fifty feet (or even twenty feet) from his belayer to a single bolt or fixed pin beneath a difficult (for him) overhang, clips into that, and hauls up the overhang has not used the rope effectively. If he falls, the protection system may collapse altogether, and both he and his belayer may be seriously hurt. Climbers may occasionally accept this risk when it is unavoidable, but I don't think they should do it as a matter of course. Better to climb unroped than to rely on inadequate protection. The psychology of free soloing is much sounder. And the hazards to the other climber are entirely of his own making.

There is a snare built into the practice of minimizing protection. Often it is just when protection is most wanted that it is most difficult to get. An inexperienced leader will pass up good placements on easy terrain only to struggle with a poor placement on difficult terrain a little higher up. Placing sound protection is often the hardest part of a lead. Often it is easier to do without. If the leader has placed good protection lower down, he may be justified in doing without. "Lead on through and protect later" is the maxim. In other words, protect opportunistically.

Protect also when it is needed. It is needed in three situations:

1. Early in the lead. The most dangerous fall is the fall directly against the belayer. I have already said that I like two solid anchors in the first 20 feet. An exception is the first 20 feet off the ground or a large ledge. A piece at the 8-foot level in such cases may do little good.

2. Where you are likely to hit something if you fall. Here it should be emphasized that broken terrain is both easier to climb on and more dangerous to fall on. Skilled climbers do not need to protect easy terrain. However, inexperienced leaders do well to "play it safe" on easy terrain because the consequences of a fall are likely to be serious.

Probably the most demanding situation in climbing is the route which starts hard right off the ground or a large ledge and stays hard for 30,

This leader has thoroughly protected an intimidating overhang.

40, or more feet. Protection is hard to get, but it must be gotten at close intervals if it is to prevent a groundfall. Groundfalls are becoming all too common an occurrence.

3. Where without it a long fall is probable. Most climbers feel that falling more than 30 feet on steep terrain is pushing their luck. They will not risk such a long fall as a matter of course. However, a skilled climber does not fall very easily. Even close to the limit of his ability he can "hang in there" tenaciously, maintain his cool, and work out a difficult problem. A less skilled climber may make a careless move, panic, or simply give up and let go.

Figure 69a. Bad alignment of protection. The arrows show the direction of forces during a fall.

Protection Systems and Directionality

The individual protection anchor is ordinarily set for the downward tug that will result from a leader fall directly against it. It is, however, linked by the belay rope to the anchors above and below it. If all these anchors are located in a straight line, then the rope may tug on only the highest anchor and perhaps also the anchor nearest the belayer. But leaders meander upward, traverse one way or the other, and place anchors first to one side and then the other. Then the rope will tug sideways or even upward on the anchors, and directional anchors may pull out. If the highest anchor pulls, and especially if the total number of anchors is small, it is quite conceivable that the whole protection system will collapse **(Figures 69a** and **69b).**

The leader has five options for dealing with such situations:

1. Try to locate the anchors in a straight line. His climbing route need not be a straight line.

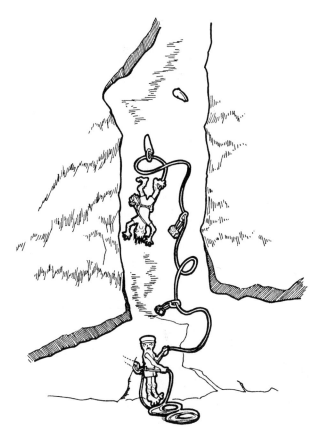

Figure 69b. Whole protection systems can collapse.

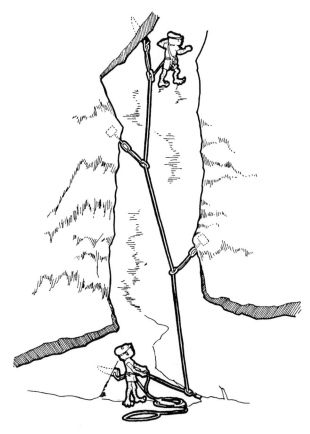

Figure 69c. Use of runners and an initial chock to effect good alignment.

2. Use runners to effect a better alignment **(Figure 69c).**

3. Try for placements which will take at least some outward or upward tug.

4. Use two directional anchors *in opposition* to achieve a nondirectional combination (see Chockcraft).

5. Avoid placing an anchor in a bad location (i.e., poor alignment).

The first anchor above the belayer is the most important element in the protection system. The leader should consider carefully what will happen if he falls directly against it. And what will happen *to it* if he falls against subsequent anchors. Climbers will often set that first anchor specifically for an upward or sideways tug (see **Figure 69c).**

We think of cracks as penetrating into the rock, but many cracks, especially in granitic terrain, actually penetrate behind large flakes or slabs which are *parallel to the trend of the wall.* With straight-in cracks, a sideways tug is unlikely

to dislodge a securely wedged chock. With cracks behind flakes, on the other hand, a sideways or even downward tug may pull the chock out of the crack. Furthermore, suppose the leader is placing a series of chocks in a crack on the left side of a large flake. And suppose the belayer is located still farther left. During a fall the rope may pull all of the chocks, one after another, leftward and upward out of the crack. The hazard is especially great when the crack flares outward and placements tend to pivot sideways. The leader must set his first chock solidly for a leftward and upward tug.

The same problem arises with straight-in cracks when the belayer is some distance out away from the wall, as he may be on the first pitch off the ground or a large ledge: During a fall the chocks will be pulled outward and upward. The belayer can solve this problem simply by moving up close to the wall.

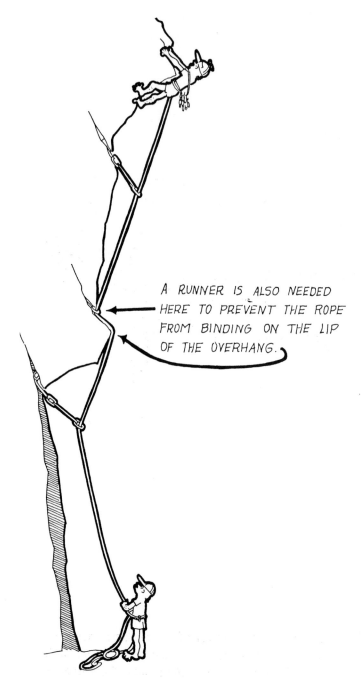

A RUNNER IS ALSO NEEDED HERE TO PREVENT THE ROPE FROM BINDING ON THE LIP OF THE OVERHANG.

Figure 70. Use of runners to prevent rope drag on overhangs.

Rope Drag

A climbing rope weighs about eight pounds. The drag on the rope from the rock, the anchors, and even the wind can easily multiply this load many times. The downward tug on the leader from the rope is also an upward tug on the anchors. Rope drag may precipitate a fall, remove directional anchors, and reduce the energy absorption capacity of the rope all at the same time (see **Figure 65**).

The leader can minimize rope drag by all of the expedients for dealing with directionality listed in the preceding section. Runners serve double duty. They not only reduce rope drag but also tend to isolate the anchors from the drag, so that even chocks perched in shallow cracks or set loosely behind constrictions can lie quietly in place while the rope slides past them. With precarious placements it may also be necessary to weight the runner down with surplus equipment or to tie the chock to an opposing chock. In any case, *it is a rare chock that does not require a runner.*

With bolts and fixed pins, as long as the alignment is good, one or two carabiners will serve in lieu of a runner. However, rope drag will result if the plane of the biner requires the rope to bind across it. A second biner clipped to the first will solve this problem. Very serious rope drag will result if the leader has run the rope through the biner from the wrong side. This is easily corrected, provided the leader sees the mistake in time. Even with these nondirectional anchors, runners are required to prevent the rope from binding on overhangs and around corners Larger overhangs require longer runners, and usually a runner is needed above the overhang as well as below it **(Figure 70).**

Excessive rope drag from ill-located anchors, incorrectly positioned biners, or failure to use runners is the sign of a careless or inexperienced leader. However, even with the best of jobs, on complicated terrain the climber may have to cut short his lead.

Keeping the Rope Off Loose Rock

Occasionally the leader must cross a ledge covered with debris or ascend a chimney or gully full of loose rock. In such situations rock is often dislodged by the rope as it is dragged by. The leader can keep the rope away from loose rock by placing a chock on the wall to one side or a runner on a tree branch away from the rock.

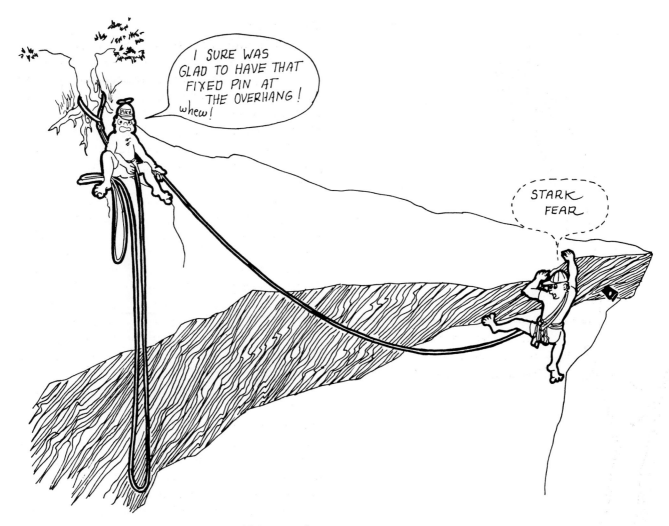

Figure 71. This leader has endangered his second by failing to protect him on a traverse.

Protecting the Second on Traverses

I know of two beginners whose enthusiasm for climbing was nearly ended by long pendulum falls from traverses. I wonder how many beginners have been turned off climbing for good by such frightening, dangerous experiences. The situation is very common. The leader places a protection anchor, makes a difficult move, then moves sideways or diagonally upward on easy terrain, perhaps "running it out" forty or fifty feet. The hapless second comes along, removes the anchor (per standard practice; see Removing Chocks), then falls at the crux and swings or bounces across the rock until he is beneath the next anchor **(Figure 71).**

What the leader should have done is place an anchor *after* the hard move or *before* the tra-verse for the protection of the second. *Whenever a leader moves sideways or diagonally, he should be alert to the need to protect the second.* This need is especially critical in situations where the second may swing into space or crash into something. I witnessed one case where the second was dangling in space with no way to reach the rock, no place to lower to, and no prusik slings. The rescue was complicated, but fortunately it was possible.

Sometimes the diagonal course of a route is gradual or subtle. However, if the second swings to the side, he may have difficulty getting back onto the route. Occasionally a pitch is more difficult or dangerous to second than to lead. That is a poor climb to take a beginner on.

Figure 72. A bad stopper placement.

Figure 73. A good stopper placement.

Chockcraft

Climbers often complain about pitches which are "poorly protected." In my experience, except for the smooth rock between crack systems, the problem is seldom real. I am usually amazed by the abundance of good placement opportunities and find it difficult to pass them by. However, you must cultivate the habit of seeing "good slots." And you must protect opportunistically. Don't insist on a placement just where you feel the need of it. Take advantage of what the rock offers.

Chocks commonly rattle out as a leader climbs past them, or they pull out during a fall. These problems should be rare, but they happen because many climbers are all too ready to rely on bad placements; they have not really considered what happens to a chock under the impact of a leader fall. Chockcraft is an art which demands both skill and discipline in the application. You must know what a good placement is and take the trouble to get it.

There are four parts to the chockcraft game: (1) seeing the place for a chock; (2) finding the stance or rest position that will permit making a good placement; (3) selecting the right chock for that place; and (4) fitting the chock to the rock

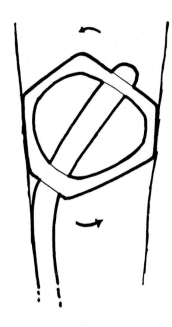

Figure 74. A hexentric placement in a vertical crack. The arrows indicate torque.

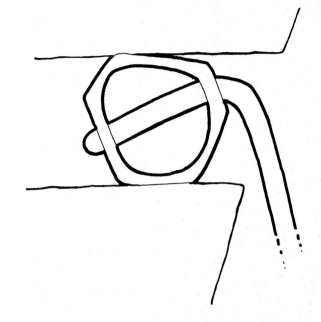

Figure 75. A hexentric placement in a horizontal crack.

properly. In the beginning you should play the game very deliberately. Don't worry about "over-protecting"; place lots of chocks for the practice of it. The time will come when you will need to make a tricky placement from a tenuous stance, and you will be glad you know the game well.

Chocks are ordinarily placed in cracks, sometimes deeply buried, sometimes perched at the outside of the crack. A hollow in the rock or shallow opposed surfaces (e.g., between two small knobs or protuberances) may also provide a placement.

Stoppers require an obvious constriction in the crack. You should avoid stopper placements in parallel-sided cracks, where only the top edges of the stopper jam in the crack. Under the impact of a fall either the surface of the rock or the edges of the stopper (soft aluminum) may rub away and the stopper rip out. Or the stopper in minimal contact with the rock may pivot and pull out **(Figure 72)**. Small stoppers must be placed so that their broader surfaces are in contact with the rock **(Figures 72 and 73)**. Thus each small stopper will fit only one width of crack. Fortunately, small stoppers come in finely graduated sizes, and it is easy to carry a large selection. Larger stoppers may be placed with either the broad or the nar-

row sides against the rock; thus each large stopper will fit two widths of crack.

Hexentrics will jam at the subtlest of constrictions in nearly parallel-sided cracks because they are designed to torque or rotate under impact **(Figures 74** and **75)**. However, friction between the hex and the rock must be adequate (at impact forces) to permit torquing. In the absence of an obvious constriction a hex should be tightly wedged in the crack. Hexes can also be wedged endways in the manner of stoppers. Each hex will fit three widths of crack.

The most obvious placement for any chock is in a crack which constricts downward, since most chocks are set primarily for a downward tug. The chock is inserted into the crack above the constriction and pulled downward into place. A surprising number of cracks constrict toward the outside of the crack, so a chock may be wedged securely against an outward (and downward) tug. This is particularly valuable when cracks penetrate up behind flakes or horizontal edges of rock. In the case of outward constrictions it is often necessary to maneuver the chock into place from the side or from below.

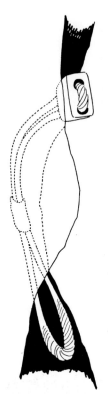

Figure 76. A stopper threaded downward.

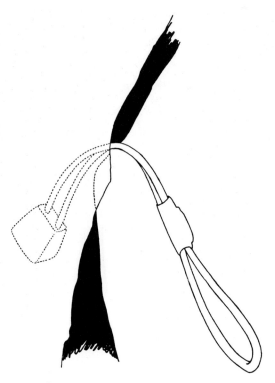

Figure 77. A stopper threaded upward.

Where a crack pinches shut at a point, it may be possible to insert or "thread" a chock wire-end or sling-end first, either downward or perhaps even upward behind the constriction **(Figures 76 and 77).**

In horizontal cracks a sideways placement may be good for a downward tug. If there is danger of the chock rotating out, two chocks may be used in opposition, tied together so that each holds the other in place. If they are tied tightly together, a large force may result under impact after the manner of a weight suspended from a taut horizontal line. Nevertheless, it may be necessary to tie them tightly together to keep them in place. **Figure 78** shows opposed stoppers in a horizontal crack. In this instance the lowest of three carabiners is subject to a tension from the other two for which it is ill designed. In a critical situation it would be better to interpose a short runner between this biner and the other two.

In vertical cracks opposition of chocks is one way to prevent a precariously fitted chock from being dragged upward by the rope.

Two chocks may sometimes be stacked together to fit a wide crack. Especially effective in this way are two stoppers mounted on the same sling **(Figure 79).** However, you should consider carefully the stability of any such arrangement under the impact of a fall.

Pitons, carabiners, and even knots **(Figure 80)** may be used as chocks.

Above all, remember that good placements are not always easily visible from the leader's stance. It is necessary to poke around corners and to feel inside wider cracks (for cracks within cracks) to find placements. Occasionally, especially at the back of ledges, it is necessary to clear away sand or pry out dirt and vegetation (with a wired chock) to expose a crack.

When an inexperienced leader has run it out twenty or thirty feet from his last protection, he may begin to tense and cling. Placing a chock becomes a desperate business, but as soon as he has clipped into it, he discovers that he can relax on a comfortable stance. It is much better to discover the stance and relax *before* you place the chock. When you see a placement you need, take an extra few seconds to discover the best stance. One hand must be free, so find the best hold for the other hand. Stemming and foot jams can provide lateral stability. Usually standing on the ball of your foot or the heel is less strain than a toe hold. The last long leader fall I took was completely unnecessary. After the fall (a forty-footer) I discovered a good foothold that would have permitted a higher chock placement.

Selecting the right chock and fitting it to the rock take practice. You should spend a few hours

Figure 78. Opposed stoppers in a horizontal crack.

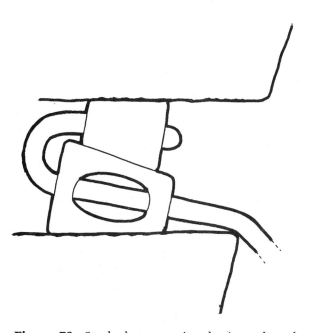

Figure 79. Stacked stoppers in a horizontal crack.

Figure 80. A knot used as a chock.

at some convenient ground-level site making as many and as varied placements as possible. Always try for good contact between the chock and the rock. Beware of the placement which pivots easily. Test for outward as well as downward tug. My placements are often canted at a 45-degree angle to withstand an outward tug (see **Figure 73).** Chocks must also be secure from upward drag from the rope. Many climbers are very hasty and casual about placements. It is worth the little extra patience and effort necessary to get the good ones.

Removing Chocks

"Cleaning" a pitch, that is, removing the chocks, is a matter of pride with most climbers. It's the job of the second, of course, and when two climbers "swing leads" (alternate in the lead) there is usually no problem. Each is experienced at both placing and removing chocks. But a beginner is usually in the role of second, so while it is the leader's equipment and pride that are at stake, it's the beginner who must struggle to remove a recalcitrant chock from a tenuous stance.

Some inconsiderate leaders make the task more difficult by burying chocks deep in cracks beyond reach of either fingers or chock pick, by tugging furiously on chocks when they place them, or by reaching as high as possible at the crux to make a placement. The leader may stand on the highest decent holds, while the poor second must move still higher into a precarious position to get at the chock. But leaving a chock behind is the surest way to slow a climb down while the leader climbs down to retrieve it, or to arouse the leader's wrath. Beginners are well advised to learn something about chock placement and removal before they go out.

Removing a chock is largely a matter of cunning and delicacy. First you must find a stance which is high enough to do the job—don't try to remove a chock at the limit of your reach. Then look at the chock carefully before you tug on it. That first tug may remove the chock, or it may make the job much more difficult. With tricky placements it is often necessary to retrace mentally the path taken by the chock as the leader maneuvered it into place. If the leader worked it into position from below, it may do little good to try to remove it by pulling upward.

Usually chocks must be pushed upward from below or else back into the crack before coming outward. I look at a chock and make one effort to loosen it with my fingers. If that fails, I tap it with the chock pick **(Figure 60).** The pick is not a device primarily for prying or for slashing at chocks hatchet-fashion. It is most effective for *poking* at them, rather as a pool cue is used. Most chock picks can also be used as hooks.

Remove a chock from the crack *before* you unclip it from the climbing rope. Then place it on a sling or runner over your shoulder *before* you start climbing again. Don't try to climb with chocks dangling from the rope in front of you or down around your knees.

The Rack

The *rack* is the selection of chocks and carabiners the leader carries on a sling over her shoulder **(Figure 81).** The sling is specially designed for the purpose. It must fit the shoulder comfortably, since a considerable weight may be suspended from it, and it must allow easy removal of the biners from which chocks hang. I like a short rack sling and short chock slings, so that chocks don't dangle down to my knees (see Chocks). The sling should be strong enough for use as a runner in a pinch.

Most beginning climbers carry a rack which is too "heavy"; that is, they take more chocks than are likely to be needed. Remember that you climb and clean only one pitch at a time. If you go all out for protection and bombproof belay anchors, you may place as many as sixteen chocks at one time. But such a large number is rare. Most established routes have some fixed pins or bolts which reduce the number of chocks needed.

I routinely carry ten stoppers and five hexes (up to 2½ inches). Toward the finish of a long lead I sometimes run short of the desired size. Then I have to be more imaginative with placements or "run it out" a little, but I figure that is part of the game, and I prefer it to a heavy rack. Many experienced climbers carry a lighter rack than I do, but they usually know in advance what they will need.

I find that the smaller chocks are both more useful and easier to carry than large ones, so I carry lots of stoppers and only a few hexes (usually the larger sizes). Probably this is a holdover from the early days of piton pounding, when we had nothing larger than the "standard" 1-inch angle piton. To this day, having a couple of 2- or 2½-inch chocks on the rack seems a luxury to me.

Of course, what is needed will vary from area to area and route to route. Usually you will have some advance idea of specialized requirements. Then you can add to the rack more of what seems appropriate.

Each chock is hung from its own carabiner except the three or four smallest stoppers, which I bunch together on a single biner. These are removed from that biner in the following manner: Separate the desired stopper from the others on

Figure 81. Climber and rack.

the biner and place it in your mouth (it is still attached to the biner). The carabiner should be positioned so that the gate is now up and toward you. Push the gate open with your thumb and remove the stopper with a downward motion of your chin.

Otherwise, each chock is removed from the rack *with* its respective carabiner.

I routinely also carry on the rack four free biners land two "quick draws," each with two biners attached (see Runners). In addition, I am likely to have about six biners hanging from runners over the other shoulder. All in all, that makes twenty-six carabiners. The second carries two or three more.

Many climbers give much thought and attention to detail in keeping their racks light and efficiently organized. There should be no motion wasted fussing with the rack or struggling to free a biner when you are placing a chock from a precarious or strenuous stance.

5

Rappels and Prusiks

No aspect of climbing has excited the popular imagination more than *rappelling*. Beginners often seem more eager to rappel than to climb. And, unfortunately, instructors and schools often pander to the popular misimpression that rappels are a central element of the sport.

Almost without exception experienced climbers hate rappelling. Of course, a single rappel down a fifty-foot slope is ordinarily a very safe and straightforward matter. But descending a long, steep wall by means of a series of rappels is a tricky, tedious, and dangerous business. It is the most dangerous thing climbers do. Most of the climbers killed on El Capitan in Yosemite have been killed while descending. Usually those who determine to retreat from high up on a big wall are better advised to keep going upward.

Quite apart from the astonishing variety of mechanical problems that can arise while rappelling, prusiking, or jumaring, there is another reason for the statistical preponderance of accidents in these situations. Equipment and safety procedures are not perfectly reliable. Though it happens rarely, ropes do occasionally cut through, and anchors sometimes fail. While the leader and second are free climbing upward, the equipment is seldom subjected to any actual stress or load. Falls are or should be infrequent, and even then the load on the equipment usually lasts only a few seconds. The climbers rely mainly on their hands and feet. In free climbing the rope and hardware are only a back-up system. In rappelling, prusiking, and jumaring, on the other hand,

the climbers have committed themselves completely to their equipment. They are at the mercy of it, and it is stressed or loaded most of the time.

There are four parts to the rappelling game: (1) choosing the rappel route; (2) rigging the rappel rope; (3) sliding down the rope; and (4) retrieving the rope for the next rappel. Although it looks like a demanding exercise, sliding down the rope is the simplest part of rappelling. Anyone can learn to do it in an afternoon at a top-roping site. The rest of the game takes experience on long, complex routes. The trickiest, most troublesome part is retrieving the rope. Failure at this point has sometimes forced climbers to take risks they would not otherwise consider. It has cost lives.

Consider two problems involved in retrieving the rope. Ordinarily the rappel rope hangs doubled from an anchor point, across which it will slide freely. After the rappel the rope is retrieved by pulling on one end. However, the climbers pulling on the rope are now a hundred feet or more below the rappel anchor. Suppose that the doubled rope has become twisted or that friction over the rock and anchor sling is so great that the rope won't slide. Or suppose that it does slide free of the anchor. Then a hundred feet or more of rope drops limply down the wall in coils and kinks. It can lodge behind trees and rock projections. A tiny kink in the rope can (and often does) wedge in a crack. Success in retrieving the rope depends largely on how well you have played the rest of the game.

Choosing the Rappel Route

It seems unnecessary to say that before starting up a climb climbers should know the way down, but there can be mistakes and unexpected problems. A few of my own experiences will give you an idea of the situations that arise.

My first Yosemite climb was the Royal Arches. I was sixteen. I had been invited to join five other climbers, none of them very strong, it turned out, except the leader of the party. The day was full of delays and misadventures, and we began the descent of the notorious North Dome

Gully in total darkness. The leader knew the way, but not well enough to find it at night. We made several rappels into unknown territory.

I promised myself I would never get involved in another such three-ring circus, but a couple of years later it nearly happened again. Six of us climbed the Southwest Arete of Lower Brother in Yosemite. We arrived on top with about an hour of daylight left. The leader of the party had said he knew the way down. It turned out that he planned to rappel the climbing route: many pitches down steep gullies with much loose rock; six people in the dark. I rebelled. With some luck and a little acumen I found the usual descent route, Michael's Ledge, and we were back at our cars before dark.

Many years later a companion and I rappelled down the South Face of Rixon's Pinnacle in Yosemite in the dark. Instead of following the climbing route, I went down a little to the east of it and landed on a tiny ledge with fixed pins and many anchor slings. "How did you know this was here?" my friend asked. "I saw it on the way up," I replied. It was useful to have seen it, to say the least. Descending by the climbing route would have required an additional rappel, rigged from a stance in stirrups, and would have necessitated leaving behind several chocks. Sometimes the ascent route is the best way down and sometimes not.

Sometimes it is necessary to descend in the dark, and it is well to know in advance what you will do. Of course, it is possible and may be advisable to bivouac and descend the next day, but unless you are prepared for it, such a night is likely to be arduous. I once made the mistake of starting down an unknown route in the dark. On the third rappel I was faced with the prospect of sliding into space without knowing whether the end of the rope touched the wall. From the weight of rope on my arm I knew that it hung free of the wall most of the way. I got out of that by climbing back up 5.9 terrain with a flashlight between my teeth. I had a top rope, but I still remember vividly hauling myself up on a tuft of grass at one point. It was a miserable bivouac.

The best rappel route is very steep and featureless except for the requisite stances and anchor places at 100- to 150-foot intervals. A less steep route might seem safer, but it usually offers more opportunities for the rappel rope to hang up. You should avoid loose gullies, chimneys, complex crack systems, debris-covered ledges,

and routes with an overabundance of trees. If you must rappel across a debris-covered ledge or through a tree, it is best to break (interrupt) the rappel at that point. Otherwise, when you pull the rope down, it may entangle itself in the tree or drape itself among the missiles on the ledge.

On popular routes one party is often rappelling down at the same time another is climbing up. This can pose hazards which a little consideration and common sense will alleviate. I once saw two people rappel down a loose gully right over another party. The two parties nearly came to blows. Using the same anchors, the offending climbers could have rappelled a clean rock face a few yards to one side.

Rigging the Rappel Rope

Bear with me through a few more anecdotes; I want to impress you with what can happen even to experienced climbers. Twice I have pulled on a rappel rope to retrieve it, and it wouldn't budge. Nothing I could do from below would make it move. Both times were at night. As is usual, our only two climbing ropes were joined to make the doubled rappel rope, so there was no other rope available to help us out.

The first time, luckily, we were on the ground. I got a good night's sleep and in the morning free soloed the pitch to the top of the rope. The rappel anchor was well back from the brink of a large ledge, causing the rope to bind tightly across the ledge and the knot joining the two climbing ropes to become stuck behind a small, subtle protruberance. I lifted the knot past the protruberance, rappelled down again, and retrieved the rope easily.

The second time my companion and I were resting in a tree which grew horizontally out of the wall 150 feet above the ground. We had not even a tiny ledge to stand on. It was a cold night, and we were dressed lightly. There was nothing to do but prusik back up the rope. I set up the prusik very carefully, using three prusik knots instead of the usual two. I doubled equipment wherever possible and checked every point with cautious, careful fingers. Even so, prusiking up a dead vertical wall in darkness was scary. I could see neither the ground below nor the goal ahead. When I got to the top, I found many old slings anchoring the rope. The smallest in circumference and thus the one actually supporting the rope was 5 mm. kernmantle rope instead of the usual 1-inch webbing. Rappel ropes slide easily across webbing, but this one would not slide across the 5 mm. rope. I cut out the offending sling, and again the rappel was easily retrieved.

There are classic tales of climbers pulling on the rappel rope only to have the whole thing come down suddenly. The anchor sling simply cut through where it rubbed against the rock. This is highly improbable today, as climbers use heavier slings than was the practice of yore. Then, of course, anchors have failed during rappels. The things some people will trust their lives to are truly astounding. I witnessed one case where the anchor sling was a leather bootlace. Two would-be climbers made it safely to the ground, but the third had to be carried away.

What constitutes a safe rappel anchor? Climbers will trust a stout tree trunk or limb (live wood). It depends on the kind of tree and configuration of limb, but I like to see something at least 4 inches in diameter. Earlier (Natural Anchors, Chapter 4), I suggested that a tree an inch or two in diameter may make a strong anchor. For protection or a belay, yes, but not for a rappel; remember that you are totally committed to your rappel anchor for an extended time. An anchor to a single, sturdy projection of rock, secure chockstone, or very large block will do. Rock features must be inspected carefully for weak points: cracks—even hairline—cleavage planes, rotten places, crumbly edges and surfaces. In my experience intelligent visual examination is more reliable than a physical test (see Natural Anchors, Chapter 4).

With chocks, fixed pitons, and bolts the rule is at least two, and three or more are sometimes called for. Remember that fixed pins, bolts, and bolt hangers are always suspect and must be examined carefully (see especially Bolts, Chapter 4). Doubled bolts are sometimes connected by a chain. Do not loop the rope over the chain—if either bolt fails, the rope will simply slide off the chain. Lives have been lost through this oversight. The anchor sling should be secured to each anchor point so that if one fails, the sling will still be attached to the others.

The rappel rope is attached to the anchor (combined anchor points) by means of a sling or runner of 1-inch nylon webbing **(Figure 82)**. The rope slides across this sling when it is retrieved, and the sling is left behind. Ordinarily, the rope would not slide across the anchor itself (i.e., the rock projection, etc.). Kernmantle rope slides

Figure 82. A rappel anchored to two pitons.

across 1-inch webbing easily. Some climbers insert a small aluminum ring between the sling and the rope; I consider these rings both unnecessary and untrustworthy. Occasionally, the rope can be run directly around a tree or limb. However, this is poor practice since, if it is done repeatedly, it will eventually kill the tree.

On established routes you will find the slings left behind by other parties, sometimes many slings connected in some complex, happenstance fashion. These slings may be abraded where the rope has been pulled across them, or they may be weakened by weathering and exposure to sunlight. The nylon webbing loses its sheen and fades with prolonged exposure to the elements. I don't trust any sling which is dull or faded. If I install my own sling, one turn of webbing will do. In the case of slings already in place I want two apparently sound slings knotted separately. I inspect them carefully for abrasions, rotate them a little so that strains and abrasions are redistributed, and check the knots.

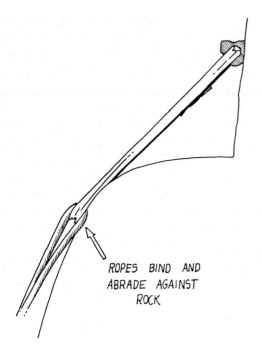

Figure 83. Incorrect location of the connection between the anchor sling and the rappel rope.

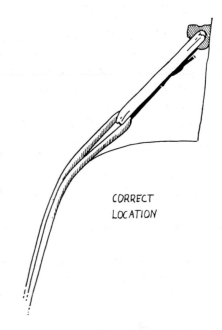

CORRECT
LOCATION

Figure 84. Correct location of the connection between the anchor sling and the rappel rope.

ROPES BIND AND
ABRADE AGAINST
ROCK

Be generous in the use of webbing. A sling which is too small in circumference will multiply the load and may bind the rope tightly against the rock. The sling should be long enough that the angle where the rope hangs from it is less than 60 degrees.

There are three important principles in the location of rappel anchors:

1. As nearly as possible, the anchor should be located vertically above the line of descent. Even so, it usually will bind across the rock a little below the anchor, but retrieval is easiest and rope abrasion minimal when the rope hangs free of the wall.

2. Where the rope binds across the rock, there will be abrasion from repeated stretching and contraction as the climber descends. Often this abrasion is sufficient to leave a conspicuous deposit of fiber on the rock. *Sharp edges must be avoided, padded, or blunted.* An edge need not be particularly obvious or acute to severely damage the rope. I once spent twenty minutes blunting such an inobvious edge with a small stone.

3. The point of connection between the anchor sling and the rope is where binding and abrasion can be especially troublesome (see **Figure 83**). This point of connection should be located in space *away from the rock* when the rappel rope is loaded (**Figure 84**); almost always the

anchor can be located and the length of the sling adjusted so that it is. Even a quarter of an inch away from the rock will suffice. Few climbers are aware of this principle, but failure to observe it is a main source of trouble retrieving rappels.

Ordinarily two 50-meter ropes are needed for rappels. One will be the climbing rope. The other, which may be a 9 mm. rope, can be carried in a pack or else trailed by the leader during the ascent. These ropes are joined with a ring bend backed up with overhand knots on both ends. The knot probably won't pull across the anchor sling, so you must remember which side of the doubled rope has the knot! As we have seen, the knot can lodge in cracks and behind subtle protuberances. Keep it away from cracks and slide it forward of anything it might hang up on.

Experienced climbers have been known to slide off the end of a rappel rope. If you are using a carabiner brake or a specialized rappelling device, which are discussed later in this chapter, you can avoid this hazard simply by tying a large knot (a figure-eight) at the end of the doubled rope.

Tangles are the usual result when the coiled rappel rope is tossed down the wall. You can avoid this by starting with a large coil in your hand and making each succeeding coil a little smaller than the one before.

The Basic Body Rappel

This simplest of rappelling methods is seldom taught and rarely seen. Most climbers think it is wickedly painful (on steep slopes, for instance, your crotch and shoulder must be well padded). Nevertheless, on moderate slopes the body rappel is my method of choice. It requires no equipment except the rope and anchor, and ordinary clothing will do for padding. It is quickly got into. It is so simple that little can go wrong. There is no entirely satisfactory method of rappelling, but this is certainly one of the best. I think beginners should master it before they learn more complicated ways.

To get into the body rappel, face the anchor and stand straddling the rope (see **Figure 85**). *The holding hand* will do the main work; decide which hand you want it to be. Reach behind you with that hand—say, the right one—and pull the rope around in front of you. Lift it over your head and onto the shoulder opposite the holding hand. Now the rope will be running between your legs, around your right hip, diagonally across your chest, and over the left shoulder. Reach behind you again with your right hand and grasp the rope hanging off the back of your shoulder. Pull it around your right side again and hold it with your right hand extended downward, palm up.

The holding hand by itself can easily support all of your weight. It also controls your rate of descent. To move easily, swing it around to the side or behind you. To slow down, bring it around front and across to your left side. To stop with both hands free, wrap your right leg around the rope several times.

Figure 85. A body rappel.

The other hand, *the balance hand,* is placed palm up on the rope in front of you, that is, the rope leading directly to the anchor. *Do not try to support your weight with this hand.* It is used for balance and to prevent the doubled rope from twisting around itself. To keep the ropes straight, simply keep your fingers between the two ropes as you rappel.

Some climbers face resolutely forward and back down the wall. I prefer to turn my body toward my holding hand and sidestep down the wall, looking in the direction I am going.

Beginners are often taught to lean backward radically while rappelling or at least to keep their legs perpendicular to the rock. No! This is silly. Keep your body straight and lean back only as much as necessary to keep your feet walking down the rock and your body away from it.

Incidentally, the body rappel works perfectly well for "free" rappels, that is, rappels through space where your feet cannot reach the rock. However, in this case ample padding of your crotch and shoulder is mandatory.

Before starting over the edge, remember that the first climber down on a series of rappels should be equipped to rig an anchor. Everyone should have a harness or swami belt and a runner attached to it for anchoring.

Getting Over the Brink

The toughest part of rappelling for beginners is getting over the brink at the start of the rappel. Usually it is only necessary to lean back against the rope. If this is too precarious or if you must avoid pulling upward against the rappel anchor, do this: Turn toward your holding hand until you are looking down the line of descent. Sit down at the brink with your legs dangling over the edge. Push your balance hand hard against the rock at your side, perhaps even pushing the rope against the rock. Then turn back around this hand until you are facing the rappel anchor again. While you are turning, feed a little rope over your shoulder and lean back until your feet can walk downward. You are on your way.

Bounding on Rappels

In the 1930s and 1940s climbers often pushed away from the rock and descended in a series of long bounds. This exhilarating method was a favorite theme in climbing films. Show-offs and uninformed beginners still do it, but experienced climbers don't.

The early climbers relied on bombproof rappel anchors; they probably never rappelled from two ¼-inch bolts. Their ropes were not as fragile as modern ropes, and they wore heavy leather patches where the rope might burn them.

The deceleration at the end of a bound multiplies the load on the rope and the anchor, and the rope stretches across the rock. Then the next acceleration reduces the load and allows the rope to contract again. These strains should be minimized, so regardless of the method *you should always rappel slowly and smoothly.* Your rope will thank you, and the life you may save will be your own.

Brake Bars and Other Rappelling Devices

The main drawback to the body rappel is its reliance on friction between the rope and the climber's body. There are many systems for freeing the rappel rope from the climber's body. These systems substitute friction through a mechanical contrivance. The simplest is a metal bar which slides into place on an ordinary carabiner. The rope then loops through the biner and binds across the bar. This *brake bar* is widely used by the uninformed. Unfortunately, it subjects the ordinary carabiner to stresses it is not designed for. Carabiner gates have been known to collapse. *Do not use a brake bar.*

There are other devices designed for rappelling, including the Sticht plate (see Glossary). In my experience most of these devices are hard on ropes, awkward to use, or both. All of them are specialized gear which you really don't need to carry. None of them is widely used by experienced climbers.

There are also a variety of unusual rappelling methods developed by the military to meet their particular needs. If you have learned any such methods, forget them.

The Carabiner Brake Rappel

This method of rappelling is far from ideal, but it is the method of choice among the majority of experienced climbers. It has two advantages: (1) It uses gear ordinarily carried on fifth class climbs. (2) Once correctly set up, it is efficient and relatively fail-safe. Its main disadvantage is its complexity—*it is easy to set up incorrectly.* When you do it, you must pay scrupulous attention to detail, and you must double check everything.

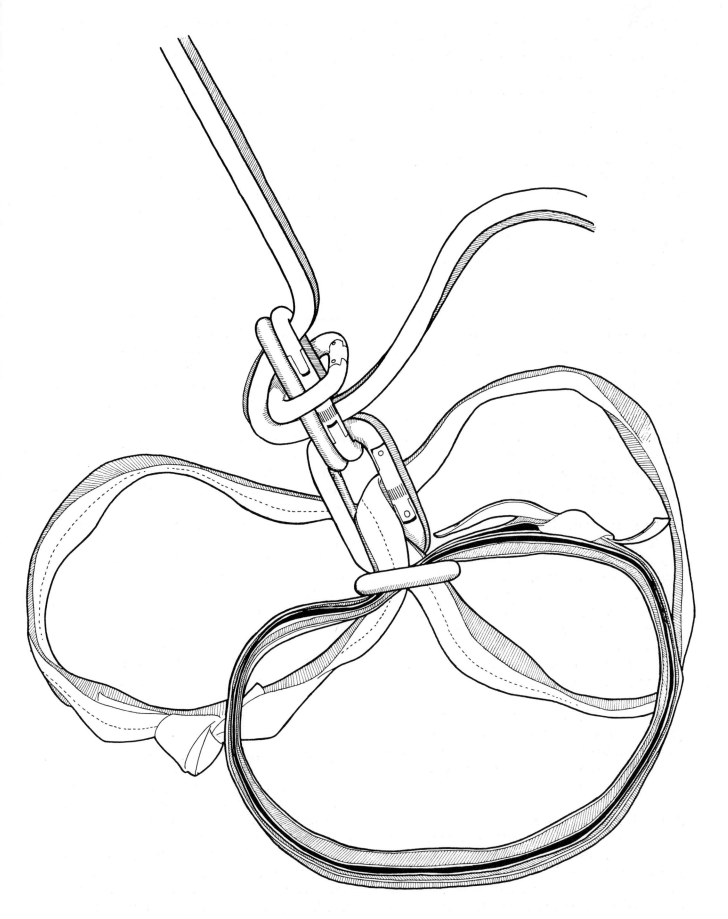

Figure 86. Rappeller's-eye view of improvised seat and carabiner brake.

Until you have mastered the carabiner brake rappel, have another person do the double checking for you.

The carabiner brake requires a seat harness and five carabiners. In place of the harness you can use a swami belt and improvised seat or leg loops. I make the seat by doubling a long runner, giving it a half twist into a figure-eight, then putting a leg through each loop of the eight. Leg loops can be made from two standard runners. The seat or the loops should be attached to your swami with an additional biner (**Figure 86**).

Set up the carabiner brake as follows: Clip two carabiners onto the harness or seat with gates *opposed,* as shown in **Figure 87.** These biners should lie in the horizontal plane, as shown in **Figure 86.** Clip two more carabiners with opposed gates onto the first two biners, as shown in **Figure 86.** These biners will lie in the vertical plane.

Now face the rappel anchor and straddle the rope. Make a bight in the doubled rope in front of you and push it through the second pair of biners from the same side as your holding hand. With the other hand clip a fifth biner, *the brake,* into place across the second pair of biners so that the bight binds against it. *This carabiner must be turned so that the bight does not bind across its gate.*

Now reach behind you with your holding hand and grasp the rope. Hold it as you would for the body rappel (**Figure 88**).

Figure 87. Two carabiners with gates opposed.

Figure 88. Rappelling with a carabiner brake.

Many climbers rappel with the rope between their legs. In the event that the brake has been set up incorrectly, the rope between your legs improves your chances of holding onto it.

Some climbers use two carabiners for the brake. In my experience this is not necessary for rappels with two standard climbing ropes and causes excessive friction and wear on the ropes. Two brake biners may be advisable with a single standard rope and a 9 mm. rope, depending on your body weight. Two biners are advisable for rappels with two 9 mm. ropes.

On free rappels I bring my holding hand around in front and place the rappel rope between my legs. The rope binding across the thigh provides the needed extra friction.

As in any rappel, *descend slowly and smoothly.* It is easy to burn a rope, and experienced climbers have been known to go down so fast that they lost control.

Note carefully: Long hair or loose clothing (shirt, sweater, or parka) can become caught in the carabiner brake while you are rappelling. This has cost lives. Tie long hair securely out of the way and tuck clothing neatly in your pants before you rappel.

Retrieving the Rappel Rope

This is the test of everything that has gone before: the choice of route; the detailed location of the anchors; the rigging of the anchors and sling; the detailed location of the ropes and knot. Before the last climber starts down the rappel, it is well for those down below to test whether the rope will slide across the anchor sling.

The last person down has the added responsibility of seeing that the ropes and knot do not lie where they can jam and that the doubled rope is free of twists around itself. As he descends, the rope stretches under his weight. Then when he gets off the doubled rope, it contracts and may twist. He should separate the two ropes before he releases the tension on them.

You may have no choice where you stand while you pull down the rope. However, if you are on the ground or a large ledge, move out away from the wall as far as practical to reduce the friction between the rope and the rock above. If nothing else, this will save some wear on the rope.

Pull the side of the doubled rope that has the knot. Once the rope is sliding across the anchor sling, try to pull slowly and steadily. If it won't slide or it hangs up, the combined weight of several climbers may be needed to budge it, although this way you run the risk of jamming the rope even more tightly. Try finesse before you resort to main force. It may be possible to snake a loop up the rope and then pull just as the loop passes the most likely point of jamming. This can dislodge the knot or shake loose a troublesome kink. While you are pulling, be sure that there are no knots or kinks in the ascending rope.

Now comes the touchy part, when all that rope drops limply down the wall in coils and kinks. Everyone should stand out of the way of stones that may come down with it. If this is impractical, keep your head up and your eyes on anything coming down. Better to see it and move your head a few inches out of the way than duck wildly and blindly into something you didn't see.

When you pull the rope to you, don't tug. *Pull very gently.* It is just now that you may dislodge a stone, or the rope may snag hopelessly in a tree, or a tiny kink jam perversely behind a flake of rock. If the rope hangs up, don't tug. Try to maneuver. Try snaking loops up the rope. Tug hard only as a last resort.

In making a series of rappels, you can feed one end of the rappel rope through the next anchor sling while you are pulling it down. It is not necessary to untie and retie the knot joining two ropes. In any case, be sure that both ropes are always attached to the cliff. Don't trust yourself to keep a hold on the rope with your hand.

If the Rappel Rope Hangs Up . . .

And no amount of maneuvering, snaking, and tugging from below will budge it, you have several options:

1. If the top of the rope is reliably anchored, you can prusik up and make the needed corrections. A kink jammed in a crack is *not* a reliable anchor. Climbers have been known to hang on the rope, assume the jammed knot, kink, or whatever will continue to hold, and prusik or go hand-over-hand up the rope without an independent belay. This is little better than Russian roulette.

2. If the rope is not reliably anchored and belay rope is available, lead upward and protect as fully as possible. Or, if protection is available along the line of the rappel, the suspended rope itself may serve as the belay rope. Attach yourself to the rope with a double prusik belay (see The Prusik Belay), which you will slide up the rope as you mount it; or, better, climb up alongside it. Using this rope, protect as you go and take a belay from the climber below.

3. Free soloing, either to free the rope or to get down another way, is a possibility, sometimes reasonable.

4. Rescue is a possibility.

Ways You Can Get "Chopped" Rappelling

The possibilities are endlessly varied. I will list here "accidents" which have happened more than once:

1. The rappel anchor collapsed.

2. The anchor sling severed.

3. The rappel rope severed.

4. The rappeller fell out of the rope (body rappel).

5. A brake bar on a carabiner was used, and the carabiner broke.

6. A carabiner brake was used, presumably incorrectly, and it collapsed.

7. The rappeller's hair or clothing jammed in the carabiner brake.

8. The rappeller slid off the end of the rope. This has happened both from going too fast and from failing to see the end of the rope. In the latter case the two ropes may not have been the same length, and the rappeller failed to see that he had reached the end of the short length.

9. The climber fell off the stance between rappels.

10. The rappel rope hung up during retrieval, and the climber fell trying to free it.

11. The rappeller or a climber below was hit by falling rock. This may have dislodged spontaneously or been knocked down by the rope or the rappeller.

There are, of course, canny old climbers who have made hundreds of rappels, but all of them can relate "incidents." Be vigilant, and back up every link in the system that you can.

The Prusik Belay

Many climbers use a prusik belay on rappels unless they are close to the ground. This is simply a runner tied to your swami belt or harness and then attached with a prusik knot to the rappel rope above the carabiner brake. You slide the prusik knot along the rope with your balance hand as you descend (see **Figure 88**). The knot will slide as long as it is not loaded, but if the brake fails and your weight comes against the knot, it will jam tight on the rope and hold you in place. Prusik belays have saved at least a few lives.

A prusik knot is usually made with a loop of rope. The loop is wrapped around the rappel rope and through itself either two or three times (**Figures 89a–c**). Many climbers carry special prusik loops of 5 or 6 mm. kernmantle rope. I prefer either the 7 mm. rope of a quick draw or else the 1-inch tubular webbing of a standard runner. Kernmantle rope must be significantly smaller in diameter than the rope (a doubled rope in the case of rappelling) it is wrapped around. Webbing is not so easily loosened after it has jammed, but in rappelling this is seldom necessary. Ropes vary greatly in stiffness and slipperiness; *the prusik knot may not jam tightly unless it is formed and snugged around the rope carefully.* Starting with the outside wraps and working toward the center of the knot, snug each wrap around the rappel rope. Then test the knot by pulling against it, loosening it, pulling against it again, and loosening it again. If two wraps of the prusik loop are inadequate, use three.

Complete the prusik belay by tying a standard runner to your waistband and connecting it to the prusik knot with a carabiner. This arrangement is especially convenient for anchoring yourself to the rock at the end of a rappel. Simply unclip the runner from the prusik knot and clip it into the anchor. Then remove both prusik loop and carabiner brake from the rappel rope.

The length of the runner connecting waistband to prusik knot is important—it should not be so long that the knot can pass out of reach if you neglect to slide it along with you. If the knot does jam tight out of reach, you will be put to some trouble to get it loose again. For this reason you should have an extra runner handy. Attach this to the rope with a prusik knot and use it as a stirrup to get your weight off the first knot.

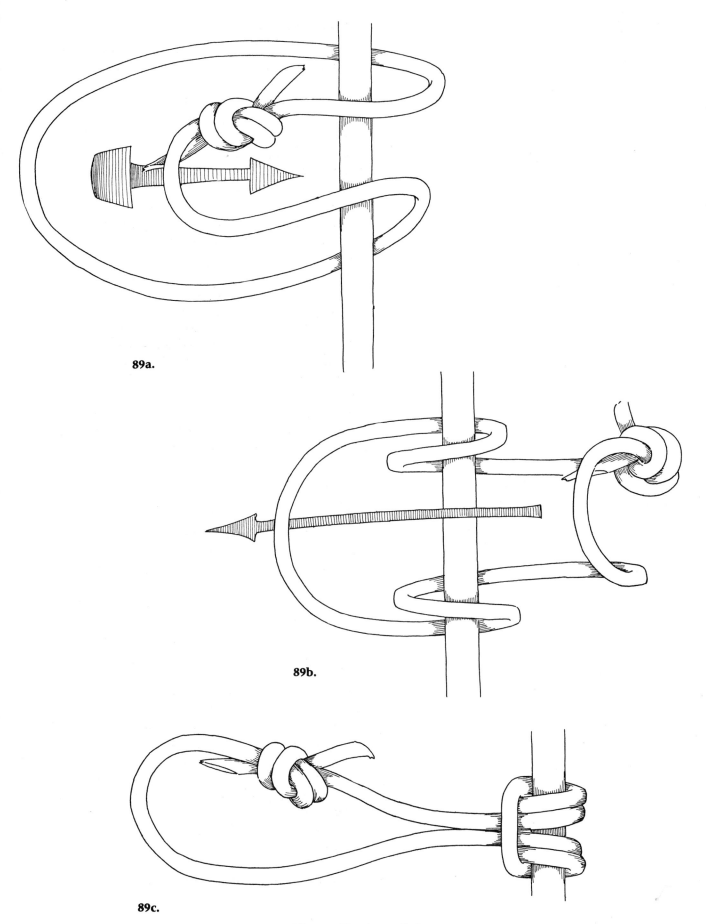

89a.

89b.

89c.

Figure 89. A prusik knot.

Prusiking

Climbers ordinarily have reason to ascend a fixed rope only in the course of aid climbing. This is done by means of mechanical ascenders attached to the rope. The most popular ascenders are jumars (see Glossary). Both aid climbing and jumaring are beyond the scope of this book. In free climbing ascenders are not usually carried. If, in an emergency, it is necessary to mount a fixed rope, prusik knots can be used.

Attach your seat harness to the rope just as you would for a prusik belay. Then make a stirrup from a second prusik knot and a runner. This goes onto the rope below the first knot. Stand up in the stirrup and push the seat higher. Then sit and slide the stirrup up. One leg does the work of lifting your body while the other hangs in space (**Figure 90**).

As just described, you are securely connected to the rope only by the first prusik knot. Most climbers want *three* points of connection. Achieve this first by using a runner to connect the stirrup (at the prusik loop) to your waist band. Then, using doubled biners with opposed gates or else a locking biner, connect the rope below the two prusik knots to your waistband. As you ascend, an increasingly long loop of rope will hang below you (**Figure 90**). In the unlikely event that both prusik knots fail, you will fall or slide the distance represented by this loop. You should shorten this distance by retying into the rope at 20- to 30-foot intervals.

Figure 90. Prusiking.

Figure 91. The rest position in a stirrup attached to the rope with a prusik knot.

Efficient prusiking takes practice. You can help matters at the start of the procedure by tying the stirrup onto your foot so that the foot has no tendency to slip out of it.

You may one day find yourself dangling in space at the end of your rope, so it is well to have at least one runner handy. Attach this to the rope with a prusik knot and slide the knot up to the limit of your reach. Then step up onto this im-

provised stirrup. You can free your hands and rest easily by tucking the foot in the stirrup up under your butt so that you are sitting on it (**Figure 91**). This frees the end of the rope. Climbers have been known to fashion a quite workable prusik system from the end of a rope.

6

Measures of Climbing and the Climber

Climbing is inevitably a kind of striving, a test, a measure of the person. I don't know any climber who has escaped the sense of failure or success, who really doesn't care about the summit or the style of an ascent, who climbs only for the unalloyed pleasure of the activity. I wish I could. I think I have succeeded more than most people in subordinating the summit to considerations of beauty, joy, and companionship. I have climbed the Royal Arches in Yosemite six times, so it is in no sense a challenge for me. I would happily climb the route tomorrow and again the next day, but nonetheless I cannot help aspiring to 5.11 and to satisfying a certain sense of style. I want to climb well.

Many climbers, especially young ones, play what I call the numbers game. What counts is climbing El Cap or 5.11. When they have succeeded, and often even before they have succeeded, they look with disdain on the Arches and 5.7. They are arrogant, and arrogance often leads to antisocial behavior, for example, chopping long-established bolts or running over another party on a climb.

Arrogance has been known to kill innocent climbers, but I will tell you about one instance of harmless arrogance. I was introducing a friend to rock climbing at a popular area. We were moving slowly, and obviously someone was inexperienced. We had arrived at a parting of ways; the easy route went straight up, and a more difficult route went to the left. We planned to go left, but first I was explaining the belay set-up to my friend.

Two climbers arrived below us. One was an older climber of vast experience; the other was his overgrown protegé. They were apparently trying to see how many routes (all moderate and known to them) they could race up in a day. Okay, but they assumed that they were the superior climbers and that we should gladly move aside so they could forge ahead.

"Which way are you going?" they asked. I pointed up to the left. "That's 5.8, you know," one replied condescendingly.

"I know."

"We're climbing very fast," he said anxiously.

"I've done the route before. We won't be long," I said.

They bolted past us angrily, going the easy way, pausing only long enough to tell my friend his belay was all wrong. The whole route is about 150 feet long, and I guess we would have delayed them fifteen minutes.

This chapter is largely concerned with goals and rules. Historically, climbers have been remarkably free-spirited, independent-minded, innovative, sometimes brash, abrasive, outrageous, even vulgar souls. Some years ago a group of young East Coast climbers styled themselves the Vulgarians and set out to break down the artificial barriers which had been raised by more "gentlemanly" members of the climbing clubs. Their activities were outrageous and vulgar, to say the least, by the standards of the 1950s. (I remember when the public display of an open can of beer on a club climbing trip was considered bad form.) The Vulgarians drank beer, climbed nude, and indulged in obscene behavior, but they also went on to establish a "higher" standard of climbing. So far as I know, they didn't modify routes or endanger other climbers. In fact, they understood the nature of the game.

Today, the popular cliffs are crowded, and there are all too many climbers on them who, in the name of individual "freedom," modify routes or endanger other people (chopping established bolts or stealing hangers is endangering other people). In doing so, the climber is not exercising freedom, but saying, in effect: "I own this route. It is mine to do with as I please."

There are in fact rules which almost every climber adheres to. The ratings given to climbs are a guide to the climber, but they are also effectively rules. Climbers could, and in the 1930s they did, spend two or three days using pitons to aid what is now rated a Grade III, 5.8 free climb (see the following sections on ratings). Today such a thing is practically unheard of. Some people might enjoy such an ascent and could not get up the route any other way, but a tacit understanding within the climbing community prevents them from doing it. If they did so at a popular area, they would undoubtedly be subject to severe criticism, mainly for using pitons, perhaps also for obstructing a route which many others were waiting to do.

If routes are public property, and if there are rules, tacit or otherwise, then I think the consensus of the local community, where it exists, should be respected. Climbers impelled to act differently should take themselves off to more obscure cliffs.

Individuals acting alone have sometimes made major contributions to climbing, but small groups in local areas have been responsible for most of the fascinating diversity and evolution of climbing. As a boy on my second multi-pitch climb at Tahquitz Rock in Southern California, I was tempted to hold onto a piton at the crux move. From far below someone yelled, "Cut loose of that piton. We don't do that here!" I might have resented his intrusion, but I tried again and got past the crux without aid. Adhering to such rigorous "rules," the best Tahquitz climbers of the period revolutionized free climbing in California and set a new standard of wall climbing in North America.

Rating Climbs

The Grades

In the late 1950s in Yosemite Valley Mark Powell introduced a system of *Grades*, I through VI, which is now widely used in North America. (See Table 2.) The grades describe the length of time experienced climbers normally take to climb a route (allow additional time for the approach and the descent).

Grade I through Grade III climbs may be technically either very easy or exceptionally difficult. Grade IV through VI climbs are invariably difficult. A beginner will find the easiest Grade IV route quite demanding.

Table 2. The Grades

Grade	Normal Time	Characteristic Length
I	about 1 hour	1–2 pitches
II	1–4 hours	2–4 "
III	4–7 hours ("short day")	3–8 "
IV	7–10 hours ("long day")	6–12 "
V	1–2 days	10–18 "
VI	2 days or more	15 + (many El Cap routes are 30 + pitches)

The system assumes that climbers on the higher grade routes will be more skillful and will move faster than many climbers on the lower grade routes. Thus people capable of doing a Grade III climb in a day may not be able to finish a Grade V in a week. Furthermore, two skillful climbers may move at very different speeds. For example, the Steck-Salathé Route on Sentinel Rock in Yosemite (Grade V) has been climbed in less than four hours, and several El Cap routes (Grade VI) have been climbed in a day.

It should be noted that European climbers use exactly the same designations, Grades I through VI, though in a very different sense—one that parallels the decimal system described subsequently.

The Classes

In the 1930s Sierra Club mountaineers devised a system of *classes*, 1 through 6, to describe the equipment and technique used on a route.

Table 3. The Classes

Class	Equipment and Technique
1	Walking. No special equipment or technique.
2	Scrambling. Proper shoes advisable. Hands may be needed for balance.
3	Climbing. A rope should be available for inexperienced climbers.
4	Exposed climbing (a fall could be fatal). A rope and belays are advisable. Belay anchors may be needed.
5	Difficult free climbing. Protection anchors for the leader are advisable.
6	Aided climbing. The rope and anchors are used for assistance in moving upward.

The designation *class 6* has been supplanted by *aid climbing* or the symbol *A*.

When the class designations were first used, they described the technical difficulty of a climb. Class 6 was assumed to be more difficult than class 5. However, ambitious climbers were soon doing aid routes free, and it became obvious that a very difficult free climb is more demanding than a straightforward aid climb. Eventually skilled climbers did routes known as class 5 "third class," that is, without a rope.

The classes thus have come to be used in two different senses. Class 3 or 4 or 5 is an objective description of a route as it is compared to other routes. Except for class 5 the standards of comparison still are, or should be, the same as those used by the early climbers; for example, Cathedral Peak in the Yosemite high country was class 4 in the 1930s, and it is class 4 today. Year by year class 5 is applied to ever more difficult terrain, which was or would have been aided earlier (see The Decimal System).

The class designation ordinarily applies to each individual pitch. A whole route is then given the rating of its most difficult pitch. For example, although there is only about 20 feet of class 4 climbing on Cathedral Peak, it is nonetheless a class 4 route.

Class 3 or 4 or 5 is also used to describe the way climbers do a particular ascent. For example, many climbers do Cathedral Peak "third class," as did the bolder climbers of the thirties, and as John Muir did in 1869.

The Decimal System

In the early 1950s at Tahquitz Rock in Southern California class 5 climbing had been pushed so far that such supplementary designations as "easy," "moderate," and "difficult" were no longer adequate. Consequently, the local climbers, who were the most skilled rock climbers in the country, arrived at the *decimal system* for rating the technical difficulty of routes. A decimal point and a numeral ranging from 0 to 9 were appended to class 5. "5.9" described the most difficult free climbing of the time.

The decimal system has been the subject of much criticism, confusion, and misapplication. Several serious efforts have been made to replace it, but it is still with us. Properly conceived and applied, it is a serviceable system, so I will try to explain and clarify it.

The circumstances at Tahquitz in the fifties were unique. Tahquitz (pronounced TAH keets) is a compact area offering many routes spanning a wide range of difficulty. The routes were done often and even repeated by the same climbers. The many good climbers, who formed a close-knit group, knew these routes well, so it was easy to arrive at a consensus on rating them. Ten routes were picked as standards for the 5.0–5.9 rankings, and other routes were rated by comparison.

As the system spread beyond Tahquitz, comparison with the standards became tenuous. Consensus was often replaced by the opinion of the first ascent party or the guidebook author. In a few areas where the circumstances at Tahquitz were roughly duplicated, such as the Shawangunks in New York State, the decimal system has been applied with reasonable consistency. In other areas, notably Yosemite Valley, the ratings are not always reliable.

The ratings should help beginning and intermediate climbers gauge their progress and also keep out of trouble. It is important for them to be able to pick routes which will challenge but not overwhelm. Unfortunately, it is at the lower levels of difficulty that the decimal system is often inaccurately applied. In Yosemite Valley many climbers have been unwilling to acknowledge that a "mere" 5.4 pitch could involve any difficulty at all. So they apply 5.4 to many easy pitches which the climbers of the thirties would have called class 4. Genuine 5.4 then becomes 5.6; genuine 5.6 becomes 5.7; and the 5.8 and 5.9 designations span an enormous range of difficulty. The beginner is understandably confused, and sometimes sandbagged; he finds one 5.8 pitch reasonable and cries on another.

Perhaps the main trouble with the decimal system is the confusion about what in fact is being rated. At Tahquitz the rating originally applied to the physical difficulty of the crux move (or a series of moves between resting places) regardless of exposure, protection, and the quality of the rock. The classic jamcrack on the Open Book was considered "poorly protected" 5.7, but only 5.7. However, here and there exposure, protection, and rock quality have indeed crept into the ratings. In Yosemite during the era of piton pounding the Open Book jamcrack would have been rated 5.8 or 5.9 because it was poorly protected. Today the same jamcrack, still rated 5.7, is easily protected with chocks. Improved shoes and protection anchors, fixed pins and bolts, and other factors, have made many pitches less demanding, adding further confusion to the ratings.

Moreover, routes are not immutable. Many have become either easier or more difficult, in some cases quite suddenly and dramatically. A ledge fell away on Higher Cathedral Spire in Yosemite, creating a 5.9 move on a route previously rated 5.8. In most cases the change is subtle, and the advertised rating may not catch up with the change. For example, many popular routes in Yosemite have become easier because piton scars now provide better finger holds.

As climbing standards advance and areas are more exhaustively explored, the newer routes are often of more *sustained* difficulty than earlier routes. An early-day 5.7 pitch likely involved only one or two 5.7 moves. Today a pitch may require 5.7 move after 5.7 move without let-up for a hundred feet or more—the famous crack on Reed's Pinnacle Direct in Yosemite, for example. Is such a pitch 5.7? The Reed's Direct crack was originally rated 5.10 and later demoted to 5.9. There are no 5.9 individual moves on it. But if it were rated 5.7, it would be the most strenuous 5.7 pitch around.

The decimal system will be more serviceable if:

1. Standard routes are chosen for each area.
2. Ratings are reviewed by a committee of knowledgeable climbers whenever a guide is published or revised.
3. The numerical rating is restricted to physical difficulty regardless of other qualities of the pitch. The rating can be qualified by adjectives such as "poorly protected."
4. The needs and perceptions of beginning climbers are recognized. Many expert climbers fail to see the need for fine distinctions at the lower end of the scale (5.0 through 5.5). However, the beginner at the Shawangunks will not fail to notice the difference between Three Pines (5.2) and Gelsa (5.4).

Since the 1950s the decimal scale has been extended to encompass much higher levels of difficulty: 5.10, 5.11, 5.12, and perhaps now 5.13. In addition, each numeral itself covers a wide range of difficulty, now commonly differentiated by the letters a, b, c, and d. An exceptional beginner may struggle up a 5.10a pitch, but it will be a rare beginner indeed who will get up a 5.10d pitch without assistance from the rope.

Learning to Lead

You should start leading as soon as you have mastered the basic skills, making a natural and quick transition from boulderer without a rope to leader at the "sharp end" of the rope. Seconding permits a degree of mental laziness and technical sloppiness, while leading demands concentration. Nearly every climber performs better leading than seconding—assuming, of course, that he has learned to lead.

Most climbers have had scary, if not panicky, experiences on their early leads, and many have taken dangerous falls. For a few novices an ill-considered first or second lead was the last. Sometimes it ended in disaster; more likely it was simply a frightening turn-off. The problem is that the novice got into something he was not prepared for.

Be warned that you may second a pitch with ease and then find that you cannot lead it. Many beginners comfortably second a 5.6 pitch. However, 5.2 or 5.3 is the appropriate level for the beginning leader. The important thing is to choose the right pitches for those first few leads. Here is a brief guide:

1. Make your first leads under the guidance of a thoroughly experienced climber. Let him choose *easy* pitches (5.2 or 5.3) which are known to him.
2. The pitches should be easily and well protected. There should be good stances where the protection is needed and good cracks for slotting the chocks.
3. It is helpful if you second the pitch before you lead it.
4. If you are especially nervous about leading, there is an exercise that will help. Second the pitch with a ten- or fifteen-pound pack on your back, then climb down it with the pack.
5. For your first lead keep your rack light. Carry only what you need for the pitch.
6. If you find yourself unable to place the protection you need, you are on the wrong pitch. Apply your skill at climbing down.
7. On the other hand, if you have trustworthy protection reasonably close by, don't even think about falling. You know how to climb. Relax and get on up.

A thirteen-year-old climber demonstrates a relaxed approach to leading.

Putting Together a Long Climb

Many relatively inexperienced climbers have an inflated idea of the difficulty of longer climbs. Big cliffs *look* more difficult than little ones. In fact, many Grade IV and V routes do not require exceptional free-climbing skill or extensive aid climbing.

Long climbs are the test of a climber's motivation and efficiency. They require the ability to move steadily and efficiently pitch after pitch.

They enforce a mental and technical discipline that is not necessary on short routes, even those of extreme difficulty. Long climbs are also the best kind of physical conditioning and excellent training for extreme climbs.

If you want to do long climbs, you should be doing Grade III routes as soon as you have mastered the basic skills. You should progress to Grade IVs as quickly as you can climb at least some 5.9 and move along efficiently. It helps to

This climber is obviously on a lead that is too easy for him.

have a strong, fast leader, but it is even better if you share the leading. This way you will complete your technical education, applying your skills to complex and ever-varied situations.

At this stage don't push the limit of your free-climbing skill or spend hours aiding impressive walls. It is surprising how many climbers learn how to aid a 10-foot horizontal ceiling before they learn how to put together effective protection on a difficult free pitch. So they "progress" to doing Grade Vs and VIs, where aid, hauling heavy loads, and multi-day efforts do not look

out of place. This is all right if the object is simply getting up impressive walls.

I think your objects at this stage should be confidence, efficiency, and technical mastery. These are best achieved on long routes which are nonetheless within your ability to do in a day with a minimum of aid. Here is a guide to putting together your first Grade IV climb:

1. Choose a season when days are long but not too hot.

2. Choose a route which will not take more than one pitch of aid or the equivalent.

3. Choose a companion who can fully share the leading.

4. Organize as much as you can the day before so that you can get an early start.

5. *Go light.* Get all your gear (except rope and rack) into a single pack. Don't haul. In awkward places the second can hang the pack from a runner attached to his waist and drag it up behind him. Keep your rack light, too. Most people carry too much gear on their first big climb.

6. Most time is lost establishing belay stances and changing the leader. Make your leads as long as possible without going so far as to lose a lot of time in a difficult stance. Keep a climber in motion as much of the time as possible.

7. Take a lightweight windproof and a small flashlight, just in case.

Pushing Your Limits

There is no reason why you should have to push your limits; it suffices to climb as far and fast and hard as you enjoy. In my view, there is too much emphasis on setting record times and on the quest for 5.13 and A6. These pursuits already show signs of diminishing returns. In the future climbers' goals undoubtedly will be subtler and more varied. Nonetheless, much satisfaction derives from exploring your limits and trying to extend them. Many people have been drawn to climbing, if only for a short time, by the realization that they could do things they had thought were beyond them.

There is a plateau you can reach without extraordinary effort. For most people with the advantage of competent instruction, strong companions, and frequent climbing weekends, the plateau is in the region of doing Grade IVs in a long day and leading consistently at the 5.9 level. Without these advantages the plateau is likely to be Grade IIIs and 5.8.

Above the plateau is a region which demands a greater commitment of time and more serious training than most people put into their recreation. Historically, the great advances in climbing have resulted from this commitment and training: Frank Sacherer's revolution of free-climbing standards in Yosemite Valley, John Gill's bouldering, Reinhold Messner's alpine-style Himalayan climbs. Today, countless climbers are duplicating and surpassing Sacherer's climbs, but few are doing it without a similar effort.

This kind of effort usually calls for an intensive training program. Here are some possible approaches.

1. *Body weight.* Most people are overweight for hard climbing. Ten pounds make an enormous difference. The following table is based on my own survey of climbers' weights and is a rough guide to the *maximum* for male climbers in peak shape:

Height	Weight (lbs.)	Height	Weight (lbs.)
5'4"	125	5'10"	155
5'6"	135	6'0"	165
5'8"	145		

Many climbers, including most women, weigh ten or fifteen pounds less.

If you are ten pounds overweight, figure to lose it as a result of training and climbing. If you are more seriously overweight, begin your training with a program of weight loss.

2. *Leg strength and overall stamina.* Many climbers run, but there are problems associated with this activity. There are many ways to run, and popular books on the subject do not give much attention to the specific effects of different running styles. Running does shorten and stiffen the muscles in the back of the leg, and climbing requires these muscles to be loose and supple. If you run, be sure to keep up daily stretching exercises. Climbing itself is one of the best stretching exercises.

I am sure that some people benefit more than others from running. If you are inclined to pound the pavement with a short, heavy stride, as many joggers do, or if you are injury prone, you should consider some alternative to running. I detest jogging, but enjoy walking with a long, fast, light-footed stride. Bicycling and ballet seem to me especially good training. Basketball, tennis, and handball are undoubtedly good. Backpacking and cross-country skiing are also excellent training, but these usually can't be done frequently enough.

3. *Middle body strength and flexibility.* Climbing makes great demands on the strength and flexibility of your torso. Few athletic pursuits are helpful in this area; yoga, ballet, and gymnastics are probably the best training. If you do exercises for climbing, I recommend sit-ups, push-ups, and any of a variety of exercises which strengthen

stomach and back muscles and stretch and twist the torso.

4. *Upper body strength.* Most people associate climbing with strength in the upper arms and shoulders. However, extraordinary strength in this area is necessary only for the most extreme climbing problems. More important for the run of hard climbing are the forearms, wrists, hands, and fingers. Climbing itself is the best training. Rope climbing is a superb exercise. Both pull-ups (palms turned out) and chin-ups (palms turned in) are useful.

It is possible to acquire too much muscle mass. Most climbers are of rather slender build. Bulk per se is useless, and absolute strength gained at the cost of endurance and agility is counterproductive. It is also possible to push strenuous exercises to the point of damaging the structure of your body. Your program should be thoughtful as well as vigorous. More is not always better.

5. *Intensive bouldering.* Some regions of the country lack major climbing areas. However, bouldering (and buildering) are available almost everywhere. Sometimes a cliff or stone wall only six feet high will suffice. Traverses can provide sustained climbing. If the traverse is short, go back and forth repeatedly. Keep inventing and trying things that seem beyond your ability. Once you have done something, decide that a hold or a hand is out of bounds and try again. Then go up and down and back and forth as many ways as you can without getting off the rock or stopping to rest. When you must rest, try to rest on the rock and go on.

Climb with a pack. Remember that when you lead you ordinarily haul a considerable weight of rope and rack over the rock. Then climb with shoes that are less efficient than your climbing shoes. These last two exercises place greater strain on your fingers, and it is possible to injure them. Usually this is only a soreness and stiffness which go away with rest. However, structural damage is possible. I think a climber should take care of his fingers much as a concert pianist does.

In all cases of intensive exercise and climbing take time to warm up properly, and heed any danger signals from your body.

6. *Top roping.* Most climbers will not do hard bouldering more than 10 or 15 feet above the ground. I am conservative in this respect because even a small risk of breaking an ankle seems silly to me. In any case, few climbers will push

their limits 100 feet above the deck without a rope. A top rope offers more scope for sustained upward movement. I have known climbers in Yosemite to test how many times they can climb a strenuous 60-foot crack in twenty minutes. The Russians go in for competitive speed climbing with a top rope.

Remember that top roping is easier than leading, or even seconding, where the second must remove protection. Beware of becoming used to the psychological comfort of a top rope.

7. *Training for leading.* When you have trained your body and learned to make hard moves, then hard leads become mainly a set of mental problems. Can you grasp quickly the technical requirements of a pitch? Do you have the confidence and discipline to carry them through: the moves, the necessary rests, the places and means for protection? Many climbers can make extremely hard moves, but relatively few can figure out a tricky maneuver on the first try. (Some get around this problem by taking repeated falls.) Relatively few are adept at resting in a tough spot. Relatively few place protection easily on a sustained pitch. These skills can be developed by intensive bouldering and top roping. The important features of this essentially mental training are: (a) constant work on new terrain, novel problems, and problems that seem too difficult; (b) pushing yourself until you must rest, then resting on the rock and going on; (c) learning the stances which are most secure and least tiring.

Climbing Safely

The uninitiated automatically assume that climbing is dangerous. Climbers are reputed to be daredevils. There is a good deal of factual support for this generalization. Every year hundreds of climbers are killed in the Alps, and every year the list includes a few climbers of great experience, skill, and international reputation. In the United States the figures are less impressive, but they are increasing yearly as climbing gains popularity. I have carried two bodies out from climbs. I have been an unwilling participant in evacuations of broken climbers often enough to wish that there were altogether fewer climbers. This book is motivated in part by my indignation.

Despite these bad experiences climbing seems to me one of the safest and certainly the healthiest things I do. Sitting at a typewriter is decidedly less healthy. I have never suffered worse than a scraped elbow and a sprained ankle climbing. I have rarely felt in danger on a climb. I have had more close calls on the highway.

The dangers of climbing are specific to situations and people: Some routes are more dangerous than others. And some people are more likely to get hurt than others. Big mountains are more dangerous than clean rock cliffs. I mentioned earlier that the list of expert climbers killed on big mountains is impressively long, and mountaineering is changing in response. Mountain climbers are learning safer ways to climb. Some of these new ways seem unorthodox. The climbers may choose a steeper, technically more demanding route because it is safer (out of the path of avalanches, for instance). In some cases they may dispense with ropes because climbing unroped is faster and safer for the existing conditions. They are learning that reliance on a high level of skill and training is safer than reliance on a lot of equipment.

By contrast, in Yosemite the hard climbing record is nothing less than astonishing. Hundreds of the hardest rock routes in the world have been pioneered with scarcely any fatalities. There have been a few fatalities on subsequent ascents of the hardest routes, but the best rock climbers, the innovators in particular, are remarkably safe. Maybe first ascent parties have more respect for the problems offered by the rock.

The hardest rock climbs are often, though not always, inherently safer than many easier routes. The hard climbs are clean—less chance for rockfall. The hard climbs are steep and smooth—less chance for damage to climber or rope during a fall. There have been plenty of deaths and serious injuries in Yosemite, but the great majority have involved less skilled climbers on easier routes.

Some climbers suppose that they are safe because they restrict themselves to easy routes, carry lots of gear, and employ elaborate procedures. None of this guarantees anything. An inept leader will wander off route, miss a key hold, or simply tense too much to climb well. A badly placed chock will pop during a fall. The leader will hit a ledge. Inept climbers will drag their feet or their ropes across loose rock, hang up a rope, or let it bind across a sharp edge of rock. No amount of caution will make up for lack of sensitivity and skill.

Safe climbing does not depend on equipment or even technique. It results primarily from a quality of intellect and a rigorously disciplined frame of mind—the intellect which is neither doctrinaire nor casual about equipment and procedures, but which thoroughly explores both the climber himself and his environment; the same frame of mind, I believe, which subordinates the summit to the style of the climb, which says that it is not enough just to get up; the climb must be well done. It implies that getting hurt is also climbing badly; it is neither a heroic deed nor bad luck, but simply the climber's failure.

Of course, there are skilled climbers who "go all out," who struggle doggedly, even desperately, ahead where other skilled climbers turn back. Frank Sacherer went all out and made a stunning list of new free climbs in Yosemite Valley. He knew that he was pushing his luck, and he retired from the Valley before the law of averages caught up with him. It is significant that after so many bold climbs in Yosemite he was killed in the Alps.

What is perhaps more remarkable is the fact that skilled but relatively conservative climbers have also made stunning numbers of hard new climbs in Yosemite and elsewhere. Among them have been people of such remarkable control and thoughtfulness that I cannot conceive of their getting seriously hurt climbing. "Going all out" can be a well-controlled mental exercise.

For the beginner probably the greatest hazard is failure to recognize the amount of special knowledge and training that have gone into climbs, even climbs which are now commonplace and "easy." The climbers who do these routes easily, perhaps even free soloing them, are not simply talented or bold. They have learned the craft and trained their bodies and mental responses, usually over several years. Often they know a lot about the routes from other climbers. Unless you are unusually gifted, you cannot safely do what they do without similar knowledge and training. Beware of the sandbag.

Helmets: A Philosophy of Safety

The great majority of American rock climbers do not wear safety helmets on clean rock. There are several reasons for this. Helmets are heavy, hot, and uncomfortable. On difficult terrain the climber may move his head and bend his neck often and quickly, and a helmet certainly impairs both vision and movement.

Still, a few climbers resolutely wear helmets. In its annual report on "Accidents in American Mountaineering" the American Alpine Club is wont to attribute head injuries to the absence of a safety helmet. Undeniably, a helmet may save a climber from a serious head injury. I rarely use a helmet, but there are places where I want it—for example, the Canadian Rockies, where rock fall is commonplace, or the Northwest Face of Half Dome in Yosemite, where there is loose rock and all too many climbers to knock it down.

You should examine the question and decide for yourself. However, let me say this: A helmet guarantees nothing. It is still better to avoid loose rock and overcrowded routes. Even with a helmet there are falls that can break your neck. Your first line of defense should be the thoughtful use of your head, not the covering of it. On clean rock helmets do tend to be associated with climbers who are prone to knock stones down and take nasty falls. Safety lies in recognizing the limitations of your equipment.

Style and Ethics

When I first climbed the Royal Arches on Memorial Day weekend, 1954, our party was the only one on the route. In the fifties I was always surprised to find another party on any Valley route. Now it is a rare day in good weather when there are not four or five parties on a well-known climb. In a major area such as Yosemite many of the routes are climbed several hundred times a year. Even the more obscure routes may have several dozen ascents.

In the fifties an especially hard new climb might wait several years for a second ascent. Today when a new climb is done in a major area, there are often people waiting in line to make the second, third, and fourth ascents. Routes acquire reputations overnight. This situation has focused attention on the style of ascents, especially first ascents. Certain practices usually meet with disapproval; for example, placing protection on rappel before doing the climb. Other practices are more difficult to judge—"sieging," for example. A climber will go up and fall repeatedly in order to work out the sequence of moves and place protection. A party may take turns at this, so it is difficult to know who led the pitch or whether it was led at all. Climbers will certainly fall off hard pitches, but how many falls are allowed before the falling is recognized as a way of disguising preprotecting or resting on the rope?

If climbing is something more than conquering physical space and having a good time, then questions of style are significant. However, many climbers simply want to get to the top and enjoy themselves. Style is the individual's own concern, and he may wish to keep that concern private. It is really nobody else's business. I hope you will aspire to climb in good style because I wish you the maximum rewards of good climbing. But you must define the standards of climbing excellence for yourself.

Unfortunately, matters of style are often confused with genuine ethical issues. Ethics concerns the relations between one person and another, or between the person and his community or his environment. It *is* somebody else's business.

When there were few climbers, most ethical issues seemed unimportant, if they were recognized at all. For example, in the fifties scarcely anyone recognized that the normal use of pitons could damage the rock. Years later it was seen that what could be done occasionally without conspicuous damage, could *not* be done a hundred times a year without severe damage. The use of pitons may once have been a matter of style; it is now an ethical issue. It affects you and me and the rock as well as the climber with the hammer. Routes are usually public property, and perhaps the rock should be granted some integrity of its own. We have a right and maybe even a duty to yell at someone who drives a piton. It is not arrogance. Rather, in many cases the driving of the piton is arrogance.

Restraint

Conditions and traditions vary from one climbing area to another. In large measure the standards of the local community of climbers should govern ethical decisions. For example, the use of gymnastic chalk to improve one's grip is widely accepted in Yosemite Valley. Its use in Colorado, however, has been found especially offensive. The residue of chalk *is* conspicuous on the rock. It does detract from the beauty and the challenge of routes, which often have a special meaning for the local climbers. Visitors should respect the feelings of the local community. Those feelings are rarely unreasonable or unduly restrictive.

In general, climbers should not modify the rock by carving holds or deliberately breaking them off. Nor should they modify an existing route by placing additional bolts (or fixed pins) or by removing existing ones. In the pioneering of new routes local standards should be known and respected.

Middle Cathedral Rock in Yosemite Valley. A popular Grade IV route, the
East Buttress, ascends near the left margin of the sunlit wall. The
Grade V Direct North Buttress ascends near the right margin of this wall,
which encompasses some of the outstanding free climbs in Yosemite Valley.

Elsewhere I have already expressed the wish that bolts and pitons be eliminated from wilderness climbing areas and from aid climbing. If the preservation of wilderness is a valid concept, then so is restraint in the use of bolts and pitons.

The values of climbing absolutely require that climbers exercise restraint. I will tell you one final story. Years ago I knew a man who was just beginning a career that made him one of the most gifted of climbers and most widely respected members of the climbing community. One day I persuaded him to accompany me on a hike to look at a piece of rock. We walked from Yosemite Valley up past Nevada Falls and Liberty Cap into Little Yosemite Valley. As we turned a bend in the trail, we were suddenly confronted by the smooth, seamless sweep of the south face of Half Dome. It is surely more awe-inspiring to climbers than the better-known northwest face. We stood silent for a minute. Then my companion's eyes sparkled, and he gave a little laugh, as he was wont to do. "Thank God," he said, "there is one wall that will never be climbed."

He was mistaken. Someone found it worthwhile to place the countless aid bolts needed for the ascent.

We have yet to learn the importance of limits, even arbitrary ones. Let us hope that somewhere in the world there is still a piece of rock that we will have the wisdom to leave alone.

Glossary

Aid, aid climbing. Leaning, standing, or pulling on the rope or anchors in order to rest or make progress, as distinguished from *free climbing*. To climb by means of aid: *he aided the route*. Formerly called *direct aid* or *artificial aid*.

Anchor. Any means of attaching the rope to the cliff. It may be a *natural anchor,* such as a tree or a chockstone, or an *artificial anchor* provided by the climber, such as a bolt or a chock. To attach the rope or oneself to an anchor: *she anchored to a tree*.

Arm bar. A hold on the rock obtained by bracing an arm or forearm between the two sides of a wide crack or chimney.

Balance, balance climbing. An even distribution of the climber's weight over the feet or hands. Climbing by such means in order to minimize reliance on hand, arm, and shoulder strength.

Belay. Any means of checking a falling climber by means of the climbing rope. A *body belay* relies for the necessary friction on wrapping the climbing rope around the belayer's body. To take in or pay out the rope in a manner that will permit one climber, the *belayer,* to check a fall by another.

Belay plate (Sticht plate), belay ring. A small metal plate or ring with holes through which the climbing rope passes. It assists the belayer in checking a fall.

Big wall. A route of such length and sustained difficulty that climbers usually spend several days on it.

Bolt. An artificial anchor placed in a hole drilled in the rock for the purpose, and fitted with a metal *bolt hanger* for attaching a carabiner and the climbing rope. Usually, the bolt and hanger are *fixed,* or left in place for the use of subsequent climbers. See also **Fixed piton** regarding the ethics which govern fixed anchors.

Bombproof. Absolutely solid and secure against failure under the impact of a fall, usually applied to anchors.

Boulder. A very small cliff close to level ground, on which the climber may make a maximum effort without the protection of a climbing rope. To climb as if on a boulder, sometimes on a long route with a rope, making repeated efforts to work out a complex sequence of moves: *he bouldered the crux of the climb*.

Bouldering. A specialized branch of rock climbing which concentrates on the climbing of exceptionally difficult routes on boulders.

Brake bar. A metal bar which, together with a carabiner, attaches to the rope to provide the necessary friction for rappelling. A brake bar, not to be confused with a *carabiner brake,* is very dangerous because it subjects the carabiner gate to lateral stresses which may cause the latter to break.

Bucket hold. A large, secure handhold around which the climber may curl his fingers.

Buildering. Bouldering on manmade structures.

Cam. To lodge in a crack by means of parts which rotate or wedge against one another, applied to both certain kinds of anchors and certain hand- and footholds. An anchor or hold which relies on camming.

Carabiner. An aluminum alloy link with a gate that permits insertion of the climbing rope or a runner, used mainly for attaching the rope to anchors. The rope may be tied to the carabiner or may simply run through it. Also called a *biner* in the United States and a *crab* in Great Britain.

Carabiner brake. A friction-producing device on the rope assembled from three or more carabiners, used mainly for rappelling, and generally preferred to the body rappel.

Ceiling. A severely overhanging section of rock extending several feet or more out from the wall. Also called a *roof*.

Chimney. A crack or fissure in the rock wide enough to accommodate the climber's body. A *squeeze chimney* is barely wide enough, so that maneuvering is difficult. To climb a chimney by pressing against the two sides at once with hands, back, knees, or feet.

Chock. An artificial anchor consisting of a piece of metal or other rigid material fitted with a rope sling or wire cable for attaching a carabiner and the climbing rope. Chocks come in a great variety of shapes and sizes. They are lodged in cracks or hollows in the rock simply with the climber's fingers and are ordinarily removed as the climbing party proceeds. Also called a *nut*.

Chock pick. A slender bar of metal or other rigid material, usually with a hook at one end, used for removing chocks from cracks.

Chockstone. A stone lodged between the two sides of a crack or chimney. Chockstones range in size from pebbles to house-sized boulders.

Chop. To deliberately break off the head and hanger of a bolt, thus making the bolt unusable.

Class. Any of the six divisions in a scheme which classifies routes or particular ascents according to the equipment and technique involved. The six classes are designated by the numerals 1 through 6, *class 1* or *first class* describing the simplest climbs, *class 6* or *sixth class* describing the most complex climbs. A climb rated fifth class in a guidebook may actually be done third class by a particular climber.

Clean. To remove all the anchors placed on a pitch by the leader. This is usually done by the second or third person as he climbs.

Clean climbing. Climbing using only natural anchors, artificial anchors placed only with the climber's fingers, or else pitons or bolts fixed permanently in the rock. Clean climbing is an ethical and aesthetic response to the damage done to the rock by driving and removing pitons with a hammer.

Cling hold. A hold on the rock obtained by pulling or clinging with the fingers. The climber pulls sideways on a *sidecling* hold and upward on a *undercling* hold.

Copperhead. A particular kind of chock.

Counterbalance. A movement or placement of one part of the body that balances a movement by another part. For example, a leg stretched out to the left may *counterbalance* a reach to the right for a handhold.

Counterpressure. See **Opposition.**

Crack Climbing. The specialized set of techniques involving lodging the climber's body or wedging the hands and feet in cracks in the rock, as distinguished from *face climbing*.

Crux. The most difficult section of a pitch. The *crux pitch* is the most difficult pitch on a route. A pitch or a route is rated by the difficulty of its crux.

Decimal system. A system for rating the difficulty of a pitch or a route on the basis of the difficulty of its crux. For this purpose a decimal point and a numeral are appended to the class of the climb. Currently the numerals range from 0 for the easiest climbs to 13 for the most difficult. For example, a route may be rated class 5.9 and its three pitches may be rated 5.4, 5.9, and 5.8, respectively.

Dihedral. A configuration of rock where two faces or walls come together at more or less a right angle like the corner of a room. Also called an *inside corner* or an *open book*.

Direct aid. See **Aid.**

Dynamic belay. A method of reducing the impact forces generated by a falling climber by allowing the rope to slip through the belayer's hands. This method has been considered obsolete since the introduction of modern kernmantle ropes, although it still may have some application. There is a limit to how large a force the belayer can withstand before the belay perforce becomes a dynamic one.

EB's. French-made rock-climbing shoes with relatively flexible, soft rubber soles. EB's have been preferred for free climbing by the great majority of American rock climbers.

Edging. Climbing by precise placement of the edges of the climbing shoe soles on tiny ledges of rock, as distinguished from *smearing*.

Exit move. A move from a steep slope onto near-horizontal terrain, such as a large ledge. Exit moves are often troublesome for inexperienced climbers because there are no holds to reach up for. The term is my contribution to climbing nomenclature.

Exposed, exposure. Describes a situation where an unchecked fall would be long and probably lethal. Most climbers want the protection of a rope and anchors on *exposed* terrain of significant difficulty. The psychological impact of *exposure* and thus the apparent difficulty of the climbing tends to increase with height above the ground.

Face. A relatively unbroken or featureless expanse of rock between ridges or crack systems.

Face climbing. The techniques—mainly balance climbing, edging and smearing with the feet, mantling, and stemming—used to climb faces, as distinguished from *crack climbing*.

Fifth class climbing. Free climbing protected by the rope and intermediate anchors between the leader and the belayer. Also called *class 5*.

Finger lock. A hold in a crack obtained by wedging one finger against another.

Fixed piton. A piton left in place in the rock permanently for use by subsequent climbers. The prevailing climbing ethic specifies that the first ascent party determines what pitons, if any, will be fixed on a route. The same ethic applies to bolts and fixed chocks. Subsequent parties may replace worn-out anchors but should not fix additional ones.

Flake. A thin slab of rock attached to the main wall or lying against it. The term applies to features which range in size from less than an inch to many feet. A flake may provide a foothold, a natural anchor, or a whole multi-pitch route.

Flared crack or chimney. A crack or chimney which is wider at the outside and narrows inward.

Free climbing. Climbing using only the holds the rock itself provides, as distinguished from *aid climbing*. The rope and anchors may be used for protection, but the climber does not lean, stand, or pull on them.

Free rappel. A rappel down an overhanging wall where the rappeller is hanging in space free of the wall.

Free solo. Free climbing without the protection of the rope and anchors. Also called *third class*.

Friend. A complicated camming chock which adjusts automatically to a continuous range of crack sizes and shapes.

Grade. Any of six divisions in a scheme which classifies routes according to the time normally taken by experienced climbers to do them. The six grades are designated by the roman numerals I through VI, a grade I route requiring about an hour, a grade VI route two days or more. The same term is used in Europe in a quite different sense to describe the difficulty of a route.

Grapevine knot. A somewhat bulky knot used to join two ends of rope as, for instance, in tying a sling on a chock.

Hanger. See **Bolt.**

Harness. An arrangement of cloth straps which secures the climbing rope to the climber's body and serves to distribute his weight or the impact force of a fall for greater comfort and safety. In the United States most climbers prefer a simple *seat harness* consisting of a *waist band* and *leg loops*.

Heel hook. A foothold using the back of the climber's heel.

Hexentric. An artificial chock with an asymmetric hexagonal cross-section, manufactured by Chouinard.

Horn. A projecting piece of rock, which may serve as a natural anchor.

Inside corner. See **Dihedral.**

Jam. To lodge some body part, commonly a hand or foot, tightly in a crack. A hold on the rock obtained by jamming: *she set her fist jams in the crack very carefully.*

Jam crack. A crack climbed by means of jam holds. Jam cracks vary in width from less than an inch to about 4 inches and are described by the body part used for jamming, for instance, a *finger crack.* Cracks wider than 4 inches may also be climbed with jam holds, but are called *offwidth cracks* and *chimneys.* See **Chimney** and **Offwidth Crack.**

Jumar. To ascend a rope fastened in place on the rock using the support of mechanical clamps which are slid along the rope as the climber proceeds. The term derives from the name of a popular make of mechanical ascenders. Also called *jug.*

Kernmantle. Describes the construction of rope generally used for climbing, which consists of a woven sheath *(mantle)* over a core *(kern)* of braided, continuous filaments.

Knob. A knoblike horn of rock. See **Horn.**

Lead. To climb first, taking the rope up and placing anchors, as distinguished from *second.* The act of leading or, simply, a pitch which is led: *he placed four chocks on the first lead.*

Leader. The climber who leads a pitch, as distinguished from the *second.*

Leg bar. A hold on the rock obtained by bracing a leg or lower leg between the two sides of a wide crack or chimney.

Leg loops. See **Harness.**

Lieback. A climbing maneuver which consists of pulling sideways with one or both hands and pushing in the opposite direction with one or both feet. The classic application is in climbing a crack with one edge offset from the other so that there is a vertical surface for the feet to push against while the hands pull against the other edge of the crack. To employ the lieback technique.

Mantle, mantleshelf. A flat ledge above an overhang or a face devoid of holds, such that the climber must pull himself up to the ledge with his arms and then heave up over his hands until he can place a foot on the ledge and stand up. The technique for mounting a mantleshelf. To employ this technique, which can sometimes be done on minimal or steeply sloping holds.

Move. A single climbing maneuver, usually from one set of footholds to the next: *the climber was several minutes working out the next move.*

Offwidth crack. A crack too wide for a normal foot jam and too narrow to admit the climber's body, usually in the range from 4 to 10 inches wide. *Offwidth technique* relies mainly on *heel–toe jams,* that is, a jam obtained by spanning the crack with the foot so that the toe is lodged against one side and the heel against the other.

Open book. See **Dihedral.**

Opposition. A variety of techniques including stemming, liebacking, and chimneying, in which the climber pushes or pulls against two opposed surfaces of rock simultaneously.

Pendulum. To swing or fall sideways at the end of the rope. A sideways swing or fall, generally on a traverse or diagonal section of a route.

Pinch grip. A handhold obtained by squeezing the rock between the thumb and the fingers.

Pitch. A section of a climb between two belay stances, often determined by the length of the climbing rope, that is, a distance of 50 meters or less.

Piton. An artificial anchor consisting of a metal spike which is driven into a crack in the rock with a hammer and which has an eye for attaching a carabiner and the rope. Also called a *pin* and in Great Britain a *peg.*

Piton scar. Damage to the rock resulting from the driving and removing of pitons, especially an enlarged hollow along a crack. Also called a *pin scar.*

Placement. A chock or piton placed in the rock: *she could not get good placements in the crack.*

Protect. To place anchors, natural or artificial, in order to shorten the length of a fall. *Protection* refers to the anchors so employed: *the leader had climbed twenty feet above her last protection.* Also called *pro.*

Prusik. To mount an anchored rope by means of stirrups and a seat attached to the rope with *prusik knots,* which jam tightly on the rope under the weight of the climber but which can be slid along the rope when unweighted.

Prusik belay. A belay obtained by the climber tying to the rope with a prusik knot, which is slid along the rope as he proceeds, but which will jam and hold if he falls against it; used for belaying a rappel, in self-belayed solo climbing, and in emergencies.

Push hold. A handhold obtained by pushing against the rock.

Push–pull combination. The use of one hand to push against the rock while the other pulls, mainly in stemming when a foot is lifted to the vicinity of the pushing hand.

Rack. The selection of chocks and carabiners carried by the leader, usually on a sling over the shoulder.

Rappel. To slide down a rope which is anchored to the rock at its upper end. The rope ordinarily hangs double from the anchor point so that it may be retrieved from below by pulling on one end. The act of rappelling, in which the climber may be attached to the rope by any of several methods. In the *body rappel* the rope is simply wrapped around the climber's body in a way that provides secure support and sufficient friction to control the rate of descent. The *carabiner brake rappel* relies on an elaborate arrangement of carabiners for the same purposes. Also, the act of rigging a rope, sliding down it, and retrieving it, which may be repeated a number of times during the descent of a large cliff: *the descent required four rappels.*

Ring bend. A compact knot used for joining two ends of rope as, for instance, in tying a runner, a sling on a chock, or two ropes together for a rappel.

Rope drag. Frictional resistance to the movement of the rope exerted by the rock, the anchors, the wind, and so on. It impedes the movement of the leader and may lift runners off horns and chocks out of cracks.

Route. An established or selected path of climbing on the rock. Also called a *line.*

Runner. A short length of rope or webbing tied or sewn into a loop, used for many purposes in climbing. Runners are most commonly made from about 5 feet of one-inch tubular nylon webbing. Formerly called a *sling.*

Run out. The distance from one protection anchor to the next, or the distance the leader has climbed beyond his last protection anchor. Used in the second sense, a leader fall is ordinarily somewhat longer than twice the run out. Also used (usually with *it*) as a verb: *the leader had to run it out forty feet to the next placement.*

Sandbag. To cause a climber to undertake an unexpectedly difficult route by saying or implying that it is easier than it really is: *local climbers sometimes sandbag visiting experts from other areas.*

Second. The person who climbs second, usually with a rope belayed from above by the leader. To climb as the second.

Shuffle. To move the hands or feet up a jam crack in the same order, that is, with one hand or foot in the lead and the other always below it.

Siege. To make repeated efforts on a route, descending from each attempt by falling, lowering down, or rappelling. Sieging is now considered poor style.

Slab. A large flake, usually several feet or more across. See **Flake.** The term also applies to smooth, low-angle rock climbed mainly by friction holds *(smearing)* or by edging on small holds; however, such rock is more usually called simply a *face* or *low-angle face.*

Sling. A short length of rope or webbing threaded through a chock and tied in a loop, used for attaching a carabiner and rope to the chock. Also a stirrup; see **Stirrup.** Formerly, a runner.

Slot. A place in a crack suitable for lodging a chock. Also one suitable for a finger jam or lock. To place a chock in a crack: *she slotted the chock for an upward pull.*

Smearing. Climbing by placement of the flexible, soft rubber sole of a climbing shoe on a smooth slope or over small holds so that it adheres by deformation and friction, as distinguished from *edging.*

Stack. To press one finger, foot, chock, or piton down on another, or to wedge them side by side, in a crack in order to obtain a stronger or broader hold or anchor.

Stance. The set of holds, ledge, or other features where the climber stands in order to rest, place an anchor, belay, or rig a rappel: *the leader could find only a sloping stance for the belay.* The term may be used also in its more commonplace sense to describe the position or posture of the climber's body on the rock.

Stemming. A position or stance on the rock with the feet spread wide apart horizontally. Both feet may be on the same level, or one foot may be under the climber and the other high and far to the side.

Stirrup. A runner or sling attached to the climbing rope or an anchor and used as a step or foothold. Stirrups specifically designed for aid climbing have several steps and are called *aid slings* or simply *aiders*.

Stopper. A wedge-shaped artificial chock manufactured by Chouinard.

Style. The equipment and technique used on a climb define its style. Traditionally, climbers have imposed on themselves restrictions on the equipment and technique permissible on a climb in order to maintain the challenge of it in the face of advancing technology. Among climbers a rough consensus exists as to what constitutes good style or bad style.

Swami belt. A waist band made from nylon webbing wound in several turns around the climber's waist and tied with a suitable knot. See **Harness**.

Index

Michael Loughman has been close to the development of modern rock climbing since its beginnings in the early 1950s, and has made over 1000 climbs in Yosemite Valley, the High Sierra, the Shawangunks, and at Tahquitz Rock and Joshua Tree National Monument in southern California. He has taught rock climbing for many years, and makes his home in Oakland, California.